From Blindness to Vision

From Blindness to Vision

How a fifty-two-year-old pastor lost his physical sight

but gained his spiritual vision

By Dr. Howard D. Blakeney

ISBN: [9781695434172]

Dedication

This book is dedicated to my mother, Peggie James. She has birthed me, raised me, and has been there for me emotionally, mentally, and financially. Thank you, Mom. I love you. I also would like to thank my Step Father, Robert for helping to take care of me while I was growing up. I would also like to mention my late grandmother and second mother Naomi Robinson who helped my mother raise me.

I would also like to thank my wife, Wanonia, for her support and faithfulness. Kudos to all my children, grandchildren, and sons-in-law. I also want to give a shout out to our Fellowship of Churches: our Amazing Church of Grace in Murfreesboro, Tennessee; our Harvest Church of Grace in Marion, South Carolina; and our congregation at Rhema Word Church in Wingate, North Carolina. I would like to give a shout also to my siblings Antoine, Cynthia, Peaches, and Michael. Also I would like to thank my administrative assistant, Kangela, for doing all my typing as I dictate this book under the inspiration of the Holy Spirit.

Introduction

From Blindness to Vision

For fifty-one years I had what I thought was a clear vision of life. Yes, I wore glasses from the time I was a teenager up until I was fifty-one years old. I had driven to San Antonio, Texas, from South Carolina, to Dallas, Texas, to Tennessee, and many other places. Therefore, my vision had to be clear, or so I thought. In 2016 when I was fifty-one years old, my vision began to slowly go away due to diabetes. After a badly done surgery, my vision was impaired. I finally became legally blind several months later.

This book is based on the real vision that Jesus Christ has given me. The real vision that he gave me to bring Glory to him through my writing, preaching, teaching, and the leading of his churches. I pray that this book will bless you and your family.

Losing my Sight
Chapter 1

The Process

Friends I don't know if it's worse to lose your
sight after you have been able to see for fifty-two years
or losing your sight at birth. I am not sure which one is
the worse but however it's probably very close. I
mention some of the process of losing my sight
gradually over eighteen months at the end of this book
however I want to speak about this process more in
detail in Chapter 1 of this book. I began to have blood
drops in my vision and I did not know exactly what was
going on, so I went to a doctor they told me I had some
blood vessel in the back of my eyes that begin to bleed
at times. Now I don't want to let one of the doctors that
I mention in the back of the book that did a botch up
job on laser surgery on my eye that was supposed to
improve my vision and stop the blood vessels from

bleeding. However, my eyesight got worse each and every month after the eye laser surgery. I begin to see a gradually decline in my vision. I was hoping for the best. I was praying for the best. One of the major signs that happen that help me to begin to understand that things was not getting better but was getting worse. I was sitting in one of my church services and I had to get up and use the bathroom and I was having trouble finding the bathroom in the rear of the church. However, I dismiss this and thinking I was having a bad day with my sight. The next major sign that continue to show me that things were getting worse was that I was sitting in the church looking at the carpet and I could not tell what color the carpet was. The next major sign that things were getting worse I was having trouble watching and seeing my favorite tv program, Gun Smoke. One of the last major signs that my sight was getting worse was I took my church on a bus trip to

Washington, DC to see the different sights in the Capital and as I was walking with the group I was stumbling off some of the street curbs because I could not measure how deep the step off was. Then I went to one of my better eye doctors and after her checked my eyes after the botched-up surgery with the previous eye doctor he stated that my vision was not good at all and he told me that I should stop driving. This was a very devastating blow to me. I am a person that have always been very independent. I am the person that have driven to San Antonio TX which is twenty-five hours one way from South Carolina. I have driven to Dallas TX which is a twenty-hour one-way drive from South Carolina. I founded a church back in 2014 in the Tennessee area and use to drive once a month there by myself and now this doctor is stating to me that I don't need to drive around the block period. The doctor went on to give me worse news. He went on to explain that not only did I not need to drive but that he was hoping that when he completed his surgery that I would be able to get around on my own. That certainly was not what I expected to hear. I was hoping that his surgery would undo the bad surgery. All I could say was Jesus help me.

The Denial

Brothers and sisters my mind could not grasp this news. My mind could not accept the fact that I was losing my eyesight. This is not the way my life was supposed to unfold. Here I am a pastor of a church for twenty years and now losing my sight. This was really shocking to me. How was I supposed to pastor my congregation? How was I supposed to drive to the churches I needed to go to? How was I going to study my Bible to prepare for sermons? How was I going to teach at my Bible College? I did not have the answers to these questions. I could not even imagine not driving. Sad to say I continue to drive, even at the opposition of the doctor. I just did not tell him. I did not drive long distances. I had some friends of mine to drive me to the Tennessee church area on a schedule visit back in 2016. Once we arrive at the hotel that they would be staying in instead of asking them to drop me off at my destination which was about eight to ten miles from their hotel I drove on my own, the whole eight to ten miles. This was in August of 2016. Little did I know that this would be the last time that I drove a car. When I arrive at my destination which was at my mom's home where I would be staying for the visit my mom knew about my sight problems and I could tell when I knocked on her front door by myself she was very surprised that I was driving alone. The next morning when we were on our way to church I got back in my car to drive me and my mom to the church service and I could tell that she was alarmed that I was still wanting to drive, however when I got in the car with my mom and started to pull out of the driveway I was having trouble getting on the right side of the road and my mom told me immediately to pull back in the driveway and get out the car and get into her car and she would drive us to the church service. I knew then that I could no longer drive. This was very difficult to accept.

Another event that happened in regard to my denial was the fact that my son told me "Daddy you need a cane that will help you be able to tell and discern what is in front of you and how deep the surface may be". I told him "I am not going to get a cane, I don't need a cane to walk." Some of my family was using the term blind and I was offended very much so to hear them use that word in reference to me and I would respond to them negatively and I told them do not use that word in referencing me and my situation. So finally, I was really having a major problem coming to grips with needing help and losing my sight and not being able to do things or see the things that I had been a custom to.

The Family

Friends as I was continually trying to come to grips with this major problem that I found myself in let me say that my family helped me to get through this. I want you to understand something, that there is nothing like family. Our priorities should be Jesus Christ first and family second. I received encouragements and help from my wife, my children, my mother, my siblings and my church family. Folks I want you to understand that at this point of the process I really wanted to die. I saw my life being over. The first thing I thought about was not only how I could be an effective pastor but also how can I be an effective husband with no sight or very little sight? How could I be an effective father, effective brother, effective grandfather, etc.? I felt useless. I felt of no value. In my mind at this point of my life I really thought that I was better off going on to glory to be with Jesus because I felt I was of no use on this earth. Brothers and sisters let me first of all warn each of us to make sure that we thank God every day for our sight, hearing, thinking, walking, feeling and touching. We should thank God every day for the senses that he gives us. All too often in life we take for granted the things that I mention in our everyday life. We just sometimes believe that we are going to have these things all of our life and that may not be the case. You don't know if you're going to lose your sight. You don't know if you're going to lose your hearing. You don't know if you're going to lose your mind. You don't know at some point if you're going to be able to walk on your own. What I am trying to teach you is to look at life from a more different and more sober perspective.

Sometimes we even take our families for granted, our mothers, our fathers, our siblings our children, our friends, our church members etc. Sometimes we forget to thank them when they do something for us. Sometimes we forget to tell them I love you. Often times we forget to say I really appreciate you. This situation that I have been going through has really change my perspective on life. Can I tell you what is one of the greatest things that I would love to see if I could have my sight back for five minutes? We have had three grandchildren born since I lost my sight and I have not been able to see their faces. I would do anything to just be able to see for a minute to stare my three grandchildren in the face. I've held them, I've kissed them, and I've interacted with them, however I would love to see their faces. This is probably one of the hardest things for me, not seeing them. Finally, folks tell your love ones that you love them on a regular basis. Hug your children I don't care how old they are. Hug your spouse, let your friends and family know how much you care about them and how important they are to you. Let's make sure that we are not taking the most important things in our life for granted. Praise God!

How Is This Going to Work

Friends the process of learning to deal with this situation is very difficult. Some of the things that I never ever thought about that would be hard that use to be easy, that use to be second nature are now very difficult tasks. For an example, my cell phone. As my sight continue to get worse I was unable to punch in the code to my phone. I was unable to dial a number by punching in the keys. I was unable to read a text. I was unable to send a text. So, by me being unable to dial a number by punching in the keys and being a pastor one of the biggest primary functions that we do is calling people. Also, I was having a difficult time putting my shoes on the right feet. There were times when I was leaving the house and one of my family members would tell me my shoes are on the wrong feet. Eventually as my sight continue to decline I was unable to tell what color my tie was. I was unable to tell what color my suit was. I had to begin to rely on a family member to lay my clothes out. I had to have someone lay out my socks so that I could make sure my socks where matching the clothing that I would be wearing that day. What kept going through my mind was how will all of this work? How would I get from place to place? How would I prepare my sermons every week? How would I prepare to teach my Bible College classes? I was always one of those pastors who not only did his homework and research, but I made very good notes in my sermon preparations. However, at this point

I could not even read notes even if they were staring me in my face. Again, my major question was how was this all going to work? I begin to think how would I get around? Would I need someone to hold my hand? This was a very uneasy time in my life. I did not understand why this was allowed to happen in my life. I knew that somehow in it all the Lord had a plan, I just wanted him to tell me what it was. But up until this point he was silent on some of the key questions that I had for him. As I continue to pray to him I was searching for answers and he was not quite yet ready to explain it to me. I guess this is where the trust factor comes in. You have to trust him in all things even when you cannot see it. The Bible teaches us that we walk by faith and not by sight. Finally, friends often times in our difficulties in life the Lord does not show us the ending in the beginning. We just have to learn to trust him. Praise God!

The Lord Speaks

Brothers and sisters in the midst of feeling worthless, in the midst of feeling ineffective, in the midst of thinking I no longer have any value to anyone, in the midst of uncertainty. In the midst of trying to figure out how this will all work, the Lord begin to speak to me. He was no longer silent. In a series of days during my prayer time the Lord told me and explain to me that not only does my life have great value that he was going to do a greater work through me in my current circumstances. He told me that eyes have not seen ears have not heard what he was going to do through my life. He told me that my value was going to be greater now than when I had two good eyes. He told me to hold on to his unchanging hands. He said that this problem that I was incurring and facing was going to be for his glory. He stated to me that he would receive more glory doing the great work of his kingdom through someone who had no physical sight. He told me that my latter days would be greater and more productive than my earlier years. He convinces me that I should boast in my infirmatives and my tribulations. He reminded me of the words of the Apostle James when he stated that we should count it all joy when we find ourselves in difficulties and tribulations. He stated too me that his son Jesus my savior, the king of kings and the Lord of Lords was fully God and fully man when he walked this earth for thirty-three and a half years and that his humanity was made perfect by the things that he suffered, in other words no pain no gain. We learn to be conformed to the image of his son (Jesus) when we face tribulations. He went on to state to me that if his son was made perfect by the things that he suffered that I too and we too would be made perfect by the things that we suffered. There is only one major way for each of us to grow in Christ and that is through suffering. I can say to you that this motivational encouraging words from the Lord was needed by me greatly. When I got up off my knees over those several days I was not only encouraged I was motivated, I was inspired. I had a new perspective on my situation. I understood by what the Lord showed me that sometimes we have to go through the valley of the shadow of death in order to climb to the mountain top of life that he wants us to arrive at. Friends let us realize that suffering is for our good. I can tell you that I am a lot better man, pastor, son, friend, family member, a father etc. today than I have ever been in my lifetime. I appreciate the simple things in life more than ever before. This new perspective on life is a blessing. I can tell you that I have now accepted what I was in complete denial about. I have concluded that I have lost my sight for a reason and the reason is far greater than I am. I understand much like Job did at the end of his story that the Lord is working out a greater purpose in the third heavens above. I don't understand it all, but I know that I will by and by. Bless it be the name of the Lord.

Let's Do This

Now that I have received my marching orders from our Lord I am now inspired and encouraged and highly motivated. The Lord has now given me a new perspective on life and on my situation. I now understand that my condition was the attacked of the enemy. What he meant for bad the Lord has explained to me that he is going to use it for my good and his good. For an example, how greatly does it bring glory to God when a man cannot see well and cannot read notes is preaching the same type of inspirational sermons than someone that has two good eyes. In 2ⁿᵈ Corinthians 12th chapter we are told by the Apostle Paul that when we are weak the Lord is made stronger in us and through us. I was so fired up after his pep talk to me that I was ready to go get it. I was ready to be an effective tool in his hand again. I was ready to allow the world to see what the Lord was going to do through a man who lost his sight. As far as sermon preparation the Lord inspired me to get a Bible by audio. The Lord also inspired me to have a family member read scriptures to me that I wanted to use and study to preach a sermon by. He also showed me and surrounded me with different church leaders as well as family that could take me from place to place that I needed to go in order to serve the Lord and advance his kingdom in the earth. He also provided for me an administrative assistance that help me with things that I need sight to do as well as take me place to place to do the work of the Lord. He also inspired me to seek help with the blind association which is there to assist folks who have a sight problem to provide resources that will help them be able to function better in life. The blind association even provided a free Jaws program to help me relearn my way around the computer and be able to go on the internet and different sights to do Bible research in preparing for sermons. I am even able to go on the computer and look at sporting shows when I need some down time. The blind association also sent someone to bring me a walking cane to help me be able to walk some on my own. This was a great help to me. I also want to let you know that I have a lot more profound appreciation for the handicap than ever before. Also, for a matter of fact I have gotten my churches to begin to donate to the different handicap organizations. Friends I want you to consider this if I had not lost my physical sight I would not be writing this book. The Lord has shown me that this book is going to help and encourage a lot of people that is dealing with difficulties in their life. I would have never had the mind or the spiritual vision to write this book if I had not lost my sight. What am I saying? That sometimes in life we go through things and we suffer many things in order that others might be helped and encouraged. When we look at tribulations and suffering from this perspective it should encourage each of us to endure the circumstance. Finally, friends I have a new perspective on life. I have a new understanding of my assignment. I have the marching orders from the boss, the Lord Jesus. I have a greater resolve than ever before. I now understand why I had to go through this tribulation. My mind is made up I am fully persuaded that my life is not over that it is only just beginning. I have a mind made up that my latter days will be more effective than my earlier days. I am going to finish the race that is set before me. I believe that there is much kingdom work to be done. Friends whatever situation that you find yourself in, whatever tribulation, whatever giants that you are facing in your life we can do this. Let's do this. Brothers and sisters the next twenty-one chapters of this book will reveal to you the spiritual vision that the Lord gave me to encourage you, to encourage us to keep on keeping on. It is my prayer that this book will help, will lift you up, will inspire you to continue your walk of faith. Amen!

Premise for the Book
Chapter 2

Although you may be blessed to have your physical vision, guess what? You can't see down the road. I mean really see. You don't know what lies ahead for you. We don't know what tribulations are awaiting us. We don't know where tragedy, or even death, lies. I have had to come to a place in my life where my entire trust is in Almighty God. I believe this is what God has been trying to teach me all of my life, and I believe this is what he has been trying to teach you too: to let go and let God. We are here by his grace and mercy.

I know that my life has been anointed and called by our lord, Jesus Christ. The proof of this is the fact that since my birth, the enemy—Satan, the devil—has attempted to kill and destroy me. My mother recently admitted to me that when she was carrying me in her stomach, we were in a car accident that could have caused her to have a miscarriage. Secondly, I was struck by a drunk driver head-on while I was riding my bicycle at eight years old. Thirdly, I was hit by a distracted driver while sitting still in traffic. He was clocked by the state trooper at sixty miles an hour when he struck me. My vehicle flipped twice and landed on the roof. The damage was so bad that a flatbed tow truck had to be used to haul my vehicle away following the accident.

A notable prophet spoke over me recently and said that the Lord has been with me closely since I was a little boy. So I understand that the loss of my vision, which I believe will return at some point, is part of my assignment on Earth for the glory of God. In life, each of us must come to a point where we realize that our lives are not accidents and that, when we accept Christ, we are gifted by the Holy Spirit for a purpose and an assignment on earth. I realize my purpose and my assignment, and I pray that after you read this book you will come to understand yours.

Take the Shot
Chapter 3

In life, a lot of our failures are caused by a fear of pursuing our goals and dreams. Many individuals have failed to reach their goals because they gave up or never tried in the first place. They allowed the fear of failure to overtake them. Fear is defined as an emotion of dread, alarm, or timidity. The Bible teaches us in 2nd Timothy 1:7, "For God did not give us a spirit of fear or timidity but of power and a sound mind."

There is one thing that all great athletes have in common: they are willing to try. They are willing to swing the bat, swing the club, or take a shot. In life we must be willing to take a chance. We must be willing to get up and make something happen. Fear is an enemy of success. Each of us have been called and placed on this earth for a divine purpose. In Romans 8:28 the Apostle Paul puts it like this: "All things work together for the good of those of us that loves God and are called according to his purpose." We have been placed here on an assignment and for his purpose. We have been called to take the shot. The Gospels show that Jesus Christ, in his thirty-three and a half years on earth being fully God and fully man, it has been noted throughout the Gospels that he took the shot.

The biggest shot that He took, of course, was going to Calvary on our behalf, to defeat the works of the devil and reconcile us with the Father. We have been redeemed from the curse because of the fall of Adam in the garden. However, the second Adam, Jesus Christ, delivered us and redeemed us from the curse so that we could stand strong in him and take the shot. So I want to say, brothers and sisters, that whatever gift and assignment God has given you, be careful to pursue it, square up your shoulders, rise up, and take the shot.

If God Be for You, Who Can Stand Against You?
Chapter 4

Romans 8:28-29 (31)

The scripture teaches us in Romans 8:28–29, 31, that all things work together for the good of those that love God and are called according to his purpose. Although I have lost most of my sight, I know that God has a plan and a purpose for my life even in my blindness, and He has a great purpose for you too. Paul explains to us in Romans 8:28 that not some things, but all things things—no matter how tragic or difficult they are, or how much they hurt, or how unfair they may seem—are all for our good. Even when we do not know God.

In Philippians 1:9 God says to us, "To live is Christ and to die is gain." The Apostle Paul teaches us in Romans 8 that there is a plan, a purpose, and an assignment for our lives, and God will be faithful to see it through and complete his work in us. Ephesians 2:10 teaches us that we are his workmanship. That's why you and I are called to live our lives on purpose, not just living and going through life aimlessly. Some may go through life flying by the seat of their pants.

Our purpose is to live and give and to be a blessing to others. Our purpose is also to be an ambassador for Jesus Christ. An ambassador is someone who has been chosen to represent someone higher up by carrying out their messages, policies and purpose. We then, being ambassadors for Jesus, are called to carry out his purpose and policies and to execute his will based on his word on earth. Our purpose is to love and make a difference in this world. Jesus said in Matthew 5:13 that we are the salt of the earth. Salt enhances the flavor of our food and makes it taste better. We are called not only to live our purpose but to enhance the lives of others.

After people have met us, they should feel more blessed than before they met us. If that's not true, then we are doing something wrong. Although some of us have two good eyes and clear physical sight, we are blind in so many areas of our lives. The Bible teaches us in 2nd Corinthians 4:4 that Satan—the devil, the god of this world—has blinded the minds of this world. Paul goes on to say in verse 31 of Romans 8, "If God be for you who can stand against you?" In other words, if God is for you, who can stand in your way? We all have problems and difficulties. We all have shortcomings and we all have enemies, but the scripture teaches us that no one can stand in our way or keep us from God's purpose for us.

Tricks of the Enemy
Chapter 5

Genesis 18:13-14
John 11

Satan, the devil, has three major tricks and deceptions. During our times of trouble, if we will remember these three deceptions, we will always fare better.

Number one: "It's too hard." Whatever problem we have, Satan will always hit us with, "It's too hard." I can't take it, I can't make it, I can't go any further. In Genesis 18:13 God had promised Abraham and Sarah a child. A promise that he would birth a nation through their seed. Sarah had been barren all her life and was unable to have a child. So, but God told Abraham that Sarah would have a child at some point. He even sent angels to tell her that in about a year she would have a child, but when Sarah heard this, she laughed. Well God was offended, so he asked Abraham, "Why does

Sarah laugh? Does she think that there is anything too hard for the Lord?"

No matter what you are facing today, it is not too hard for God. Goliath was not too big for David to defeat. The Red Sea was not too deep for God to part. The furnace was not too hot for God to deliver the Hebrew boys. The lion's mouth was not too strong for God to save Daniel. Your problem is not too hard for God. If God can cause Sarah to have a newborn baby in her nineties, nothing is too hard for God. Trust him. Amen!

The next deception that the enemy wants us to believe when we are facing trouble is that what you have is too little. You don't have enough resources to stand through this circumstance. You don't have enough strength, help, or enough money. In the book of Matthew, Jesus had just learned of the death of his cousin John the Baptist. The multitude had gathered in a remote area, and Jesus took a boat over to them. The Bible indicates that there were fifteen thousand men, women, and children. The people were hungry, and Jesus told the disciples to feed them.

The disciples, who often acted just like you or I would, said, "Jesus we don't have enough resources for this circumstance, for this problem." They said, "We don't have enough. We only have two fish and five loaves of bread." What did Jesus do? He took the food, and blessed it, and then gave it to the disciples to distribute to the people. The Bible says that all fifteen thousand of them were filled and there was some food left over.

God is more than enough for whatever problem in life that you are facing. Don't allow the enemy to tell you any different. Jesus is the God of more than enough.

The third deception is that the enemy wants us to believe is that when we are facing trouble, it's too late to do anything about it. It's too late for the problem to be fixed or resolved. He wants us to think there is no chance. Jesus had a good friend called Lazarus. When Lazarus became ill, his sister sent for Jesus. When Jesus heard Lazarus was sick, he stayed in the same place for two more days. By the time Jesus reached Lazarus, he was dead.

We can learn from this last statement that God's timing is not always ours. God does not move in our life by our watch. He has his own watch and timing, and as some of our older matriarchs and patriarchs have said, "He may not always come when we think he should, but he is always on time."

When Jesus arrived, one of the sisters was very upset with him because Lazarus had already died. She said that if Jesus would have come sooner, her brother would have not died. Isn't that how you and I feel at times? If God would just hurry up and come as soon as we call on him, our situation would be better. Or would it be?

Jesus asked them to take him to the tomb where they had buried Lazarus. The sisters thought that it was already too late for anything to be done about their profound trouble. The sisters tried to that explain that to Jesus. Jesus said to them, "It's never too late when I am involved. It's never too late if you trust in me."

By this time Lazarus had been dead for three days and was stinking. He was in the grave. His body had started to decay. Most people would say it was too late. Jesus said, "Lazarus come forth," and Lazarus was resurrected back to life. In other words, brothers and sisters, no matter how much the enemy tells us that our circumstances are hopeless, Jesus the Christ is always able to raise up what is dead in our lives.

The Assignment
Chapter 6

In Jeremiah 1:5, the Lord tells us that from the time that we are in our mother's womb, he not only knows us, he has a purpose for our life. He has given us a role and an assignment on earth and provides us with spiritual gifts in order to carry out his divine purpose. That is why some people communicate better than others. Some have been given more gifts than others.

The Parable of the Talents begins in Matthew 25 beginning at verse 14. The owner in the parable represents God the Father, and according to this parable He gives us spiritual gifts in order to accomplish his kingdom's purpose on the earth. All too often those of us that are in the body of Christ sometimes are slothful in using what God gives us to accomplish his purpose. We bury the gifts that he gives us. Some of us are just plain spiritually and physically lazy. That is why, while some of us are like the individuals in the parable who doubled the talents the owner had given them, some of us are like the person who made an excuse for not getting it done. Therefore, we live a life that is unproductive for the kingdom.

Some us have the attitudes of the first two individuals—that we are going to get it done for the kingdom with God's help, no matter the cost. But others are like the third individual in the parable that procrastinates, and they never allow themselves to be an effective tool in the hands of the Lord. Many of us allow the cares and concerns of this world to take us off the assignments that the Lord has given us. Some of us are laser focused on our assignments, much like the first two individuals in the parable.

When I became legally blind a little over two years ago, I learned that there is an uncertainty when you eat because you cannot see what you are eating. There is also uncertainty when you go to the bathroom because you have to feel your way to that destination. The Lord has given me a very difficult task: to write a book that I cannot physically see. However, Glory be to God that I am able to see in the spirit. I write this book under the inspiration of the Holy Spirit.

In Ecclesiastes 9:10, King Solomon was inspired by the Holy spirit. Whatever you decide to do in life give it everything that you have. Whatever you are given to become in this life, do it with everything you have for the glory of Jesus. If you get married, be the best husband. If you decide to have children, be the best parent that you can be. If you decide to serve God, then serve him with everything you have.

Be the best employee, employer, sister, brother, neighbor, grandparent, or whoever you are in life, because God says a time is coming when you and I will not be able to serve. Eventually we will die, and some of us will get old enough that we will not be able to do the things that we do now. So let's serve God's people and our community while we can. God the Father has given us all a purpose and an assignment on earth. He gave some of us the gift of preaching, some teaching, some attorneys, some physical therapists, nurses, bankers etc. What are doing with your gift? What have you done with the gift that God gave you? Have you used it? Have you used it to bless others or are you sitting on it? Have you failed to use it? Have you been lazy or slothful?

The good news is that no matter how lazy or slothful you have been in the past, you can now make this a new beginning. Start today. If your gift is singing, sing. If your gift is teaching, teach. If your gift is writing, write. If your gift is doctoring than do so. If your gift is serving children, then serve. If your gift is helping people with autism, then help. If your gift is feeding the poor, then feed.

In closing, let's be sure to be like the first two individuals in the Parable of the Talents. Let's get off our backsides and utilize whatever gifts and talents that the Lord has given us. Let's be careful to use them for his purpose and to complete our assignments on earth. Amen!

Living in Babylon
Chapter 7

Brothers and sisters, in the book of Daniel, the Prophet

Daniel and the Hebrew boys and the Nation of Israel

were taken into captivity by King Nebuchadnezzar. The

system that held them captive was a system that had

traditions and a lifestyle different than Israel's. They

had false gods, pagan gods, and traditions of eating and

drinking that were far from the God that the Israelites

served—the God of Abraham, Isaac, and Jacob.

Brothers and sisters, we are living today in the same

pagan, Babylonian system that the Prophet Daniel lived

in thousands of years ago. This system, much like

theirs, influences us to live and think in a far different

way than our Lord Jesus Christ expects us to live and

think. The false system teaches us that there is no God

and that we should live any old way that we want to.

The Bible teaches us that in 2 Corinthians 4 that Satan,

the devil, is the god of this world, is in control of this

world, and influences the minds of the people that live on Earth. Much like in the days of the Prophet Daniel and the Hebrew boys, this nation has taken Jesus out of everything, including our schools, government, our communities, our homes, marriages, families, and even our churches.

King Nebuchadnezzar decided to place the Hebrew boys in the fiery furnace that was hotter than hot because they refused to live the lifestyle of Babylon. The Hebrew boys knew and trusted in God because they knew he had the power to deliver them if he chose to. This Babylonian, anti-god system has now been carried over to the twenty-first century. Although most people do not realize it, we are currently living in a system like Babylon, is anti-god, anti-Christian and anti-Jesus. Jesus even foretold of this time in Matthew 24. He said that love would wax cold and evil would run rampant. In 2nd Timothy 3:1, Paul told Timothy that perilous times of difficulty would come in the latter days.

Brothers and sisters, we are currently living in a nation where Christians have become second class citizens. Now the word Christian has become a bad word to the false spiritual system that we live in. This was no different than in the days of Daniel and the Hebrew boys. The question is, will we stand up like the Prophet Daniel and Hebrew boys and refuse to bow to the false modern-day Babylonian system? Will we buy into the philosophy of this Babylonian system? Will we stand up for Gods' way or will we sub come to the way of the satanic system? Paul hit the nail on the head when he said they would call evil good. We are living in a time of political chaos. I am neither a democrat nor a Republican. However, I am Jesuscan and Jesuscratic.

Sometimes I have voted republican and sometimes I have voted democratic, however I vote for the person whose policies and views align more closely with the word of God.

Brothers and sisters, we are called to stand up and take a stand. One wise man said, "If you don't stand for something you will fall for anything." This is why every day we only need to look at the news to see how bad our nation has become, with things such as school shootings, people being gunned down on the streets, and parents murdering babies. This Babylonian system is the opposite of God's word. Day by day, week by week, month by month the moral fabric of this nation is being ripped apart. However, we are called to stand like Daniel did. Like the Hebrew boys and Jesus did. In John 17, Jesus said that we are to be in the world but not of the world. In Romans 12:2, the Apostle Paul put it like this: our minds are to be transformed and renewed day by day, and the only way to do this is to study the word of God, which washes us clean.

The Bible teaches in the book of Proverbs that the word of God is a lamp unto our feet. We are not to lean on our own understanding but in all our ways acknowledge him (Jesus). Let's take a stand and trust Jesus Christ to take care of us and provide for us, like he did for Daniel. The devil is always trying to put us in the fiery furnace of difficulty and tribulation. Like God delivered them, he will deliver us.

King Nebuchadnezzar had them turn the heat on the fiery furnace way up in attempt to destroy the Hebrew boys, just like Satan and his system are always turning up the heat of difficulty in our lives. But our God is faithful to see us through. Just stand, even when you don't feel like it. Even when things get tough, just stand and watch the Lord deliver us from the fiery furnace.

In closing, there is a literal kingdom that is coming, and there will be a just and fair system where every tongue will confess, and every knee will bow to the King of Kings and Lord of Lords, Jesus Christ. In Matthew 24:14, Jesus said that the end of this world would not come until the Gospel of the kingdom had been preached throughout the world. In Isaiah 9:6, the Prophet Isaiah stated that the coming government of the kingdom of God would be upon the shoulders of Jesus. Jesus is just. He will govern with justice and true equality because he is perfect. Think of it—no more political ads, no more smear campaigns, no more tragic shootings, no more diseases cutting lives short, no more cancer, no more diabetes, no more tragic auto accidents or airplane crashes. The Bible says death will be swallowed up. Oh death, where is thy sting? Oh grave, where is thou victory? We will be given spiritual bodies that are not subject to decay or diseases. 1st Corinthians 15:45–50 says Jesus will be king over all the earth. He will be president of the world. At that time, every knee will bow, and every tongue will confess that Jesus is Lord (Phil. 2:10-11) In other words, friend hold on, because help is on the way. In Jesus's name!

Uncomfortable Obedience
Chapter 8

Genesis 22:1-3

Brothers and sisters, often times obedience to the Lord is not comfortable. The problem is that we find ourselves going against the word of God and the will of God, because it does not fit what we want to do or what we feel like we need to do.

Here in this storyline, we find the father of the faithful, Abraham, is asked by God to do something that is very uncomfortable. The first thing that we can learn from this story is that God tests us. Although Abraham had displayed obedience prior to this storyline, here in Genesis 22, God again tested Abraham. The first thing that we learn here is that the Lord tests us so we can grow. Satan tempts us to destroy us. Oftentimes when God tests us, what he asks us to do makes no human sense. But the Bible teaches us that the Lord's ways and thoughts are as high over our ways and thoughts as the heaven is above the earth.

When the children of Israel were led out of Egypt after four hundred and thirty years of slavery and bondage, they found themselves with their backs against the Red Sea, and the most powerful military on the earth at the time was charging against them. Did this mean that the Lord was a terrible floor general? The answer is no. God always does everything for a purpose. When he tests us in our everyday lives, it is for a purpose. Although we may not understand, it is for a purpose.

In Romans 8:28, the Apostle Paul put it like this: "All things work together for the good for those that love God and are called according to his purpose." Here in the story, Abraham had been asked by God to sacrifice his son that was the promised seed. God did not explain why, he did not give Abraham the details for its purpose. He just asked him to take his son Isaac to a mountain and present him as a sacrifice on the altar.

Now Abraham had to be thinking, "Lord you promised me this son when I was seventy years old and my wife Sarah was barren. You delivered the child to me at the age of ninety-nine. You promised me that our descendants would be as many as the stars. And now you're asking me to take that promised seed that came twenty-nine years after that promise and sacrifice him on an altar." You can imagine, brothers and sisters, what had to be going through the mind of Abraham. This makes no human sense. How many times has God asked you, through his word and through the preaching of his ministers, to do something, turn away from something, or give someone or something up that disturbs you and hurts you so badly that it becomes very uncomfortable. This is often why we disobey—

because what God asks us to do when he is testing us at times makes no human sense and/or does not line up with what we want to do.

Although Abraham did not understand why God would ask him to sacrifice the promised son, he got up, the Bible says, and did what God asked him to do. So we can learn the following from the father of the faithful.

Number one: when God asks us to obey and when he tests us, it will not always make human sense. It made no sense for a young shepherd boy to fight a nine-and-a-half foot giant called Goliath. It made no sense for the Hebrew boys to be thrown in the fiery furnace just because they wanted to obey God. It made no human sense for a man called Saul to be struck down on the road to Damascus, then be converted to an apostle after throwing Christians into jail and persecuting them. It made no human sense for Jesus

Christ to visit the home of Zacchaeus who was a chief tax collector, one of the most hated types of individual in Jesus's time. In my personal situation, it made no human sense for a successful pastor, after twenty years in the ministry, to lose my sight but still be asked by God to fulfill the assignment that he had given me.

What is it in your life that God is asking you to do or to give up in order to execute his will? What is it that is causing you to be very uncomfortable in your life, lining it up with the word of God? Abraham got up and went to the mountain that God told him to in order to make the sacrifice. In the latter part of Genesis 22, Abraham took his son Isaac laid him on the altar, tied him down, took the knife, raised the knife with two hands above his head to slay his son like God said to. But then the angel shouted out to him, "Stop Abraham. Don't lay a hand on your son. Now I know that you will not withhold anything from me."

In other words, God was saying, "No matter what I ask you to do, you will do it."

What about us? What about you?

This scene was a forerunner of what was to come. Abraham here represents the father in heaven, and Isaac represents the Son Jesus. Isaac is lying there to be sacrificed, not even fighting against it, allowing his father to bind him with no fight or opposition. The son here is a symbol for Jesus laying down his life because the Father asked him to. From the mountain in this scene, you can look over and see a view of Cavalry, where Jesus would be sacrificed in willing obedience to the Father several hundred years later. Our last point regarding uncomfortable obedience is in the twenty-sixth chapter of Matthew. The son Jesus was in the garden of Gethsemane immediately prior to going to Calvary to be sacrificed, and his humanity began to cry out. He asked his father in heaven, is there any other way than for me to go to the cross? Remember he had lived from the beginning with his father in heaven in perfect harmony. He had never been struck. He had never been beaten. He had never been betrayed, and now he was about to suffer the most grueling death that any human since the beginning of time had ever suffered. The Bible teaches us that while he was in prayer to the Father in the garden, he sweat drops of blood. This reveals to us how intense his experience was. All of the sins of the world since the beginning of time and until the end of time were upon his shoulders.

Jesus was being sacrificed to redeem all of humanity from the fall of Adam in the garden of Eden. No other human had lived a life without blemish; the Bible teaches us that this lamb had to be without sin to be fit to cover the sins of mankind. No prophet nor apostle had lived a sinless life. However, when Jesus asked the Father if there was any other way that this cup may pass from him, he quickly followed his request with "nevertheless thy will be done." It is an understatement to say that this was uncomfortable obedience. Let us, as we live our lives each day, keep in mind that the Lord tests us so we can grow. No wonder the Apostle James tells us to count it all joy when we find ourselves in difficulty and tribulation. And what James understood was that all the difficulties in which we find ourselves, God has permitted so we can grow. Let us, as we face test each day in our lives, be quick to obey, realizing that we don't have to understand everything to be obedient. Let's be like Abraham and Jesus. Let's trust in the God of the universe. Let's trust in the one that makes no mistakes. Let's trust in the God of Abraham, Isaac, and Jacob. Let's just do it.

Prayer: The Real Battleground
Chapter 9

Mark 1:35

In Ephesian 6:12, the Apostle Paul reminds each of us that our struggles and our wars are not against each other. He says, "For we wrestle not against flesh and blood but against wickedness and darkness in high places." Jesus Christ understood this during his thirty-three and half years on earth. This was the reason he was able to withstand the attacks of the Pharisees, a religious and political group that oftentimes tried to make his life a living Hell. Satan the devil came against Jesus on every opportunity that he could, but I say to you that the way that Jesus was able to withstand his enemies and oppositions and wickedness in high places was on the battleground of prayer.

Prayer is an intimate dialogue between a man or a woman and God. You do not have to be on your knees each time to pray. In the book of Job as we look at the story, we find that even though Job faced many disturbing tragedies, he was able to get through them all and eventually be restored to even more than he had before. This was all due to his relationship and constant communication with God. It is impossible to know God in an intimate way without a very good prayer life. You show me someone that does not have a good, persistent prayer life, and I will show you someone that is losing a battle to Satan each and every day.

When you see someone that is living in constant sin, that person does not have an intimate prayer life. It is impossible to live in a repetitively sinful way and yet be in prayer with the creator of the universe. In Mark 1:35, we see that Jesus left his disciples, as was his practice early in the day, then went to a quiet place by himself with no distractions and prayed to his father in heaven. This is how he was able to withstand the attacks of the enemy. We also learn in this story that we must create a war room within our homes. We must establish a place of prayer for ourselves that has no distractions and where there is no one around. This is the only way we will be able to tune out the busyness of life and the distractions that the enemy throws at us daily.

It is a tragedy to create so much busyness in our lives that we are distracted from the assignment that Jesus has given us on earth. Prayer, the real battleground, brings us back into the intimacy of our relationship with Jesus Christ. It also is a place where we can not only communicate to him but also can hear from him. In order to give us the guidance and the directions in our lives that we need from him. We can pray while we walk for exercise, while we drive our cars to work, and most optimally when we go into our war rooms where we establish quiet times with him. The Bible teaches us to pray without ceasing and to make our petitions known to Jesus. We should even study the word of God while on our knees in prayer. We cannot win our daily battles of difficulties without the proper intimacy with God in prayer. One preacher once described prayer using the word PUSH—Pray Until Something Happens.

In second Chronicles 7:14 the writer says, "If my people who are called by my name will pray and humble themselves and turn from their wicked ways, I will heal the land." In the passage, God describes how to get intimate with him. The Lord says that the way to get something in our lives to turn around begins with prayer. These instructions for making a change for the better leads with prayer and then humbling ourselves in the sight of God. Prayer is the number one way to be intimate with God. The word intimate means in-to-me. God is asking us to come in-to-me or in-to-him.

People often say, "I don't have time to pray," but the great theologian Martin Luther said we don't have time *not* to pray. Notice in the passage from Mark that Jesus begins his day with prayer. When we begin our day with prayer, we are saying to God that we need him today. We cannot handle today without his presence. When we begin a day without prayer, we are saying to God, "I got this. I can handle today without your help". So brothers and sisters, let's begin each day in our war rooms by having an intimate conversation with Jesus Christ. Let's let God know that we need him all day every day. Let's use prayer like Jesus did to grow in our relationship and intimacy with the Father. Let's lay aside every distraction as we talk and speak and communicate with Jesus. Let's realize that prayer is an intimate act with God and that it is the real battleground.

Getting off the Dock
Chapter 10

The great blues singer Otis Redding had a very famous song that went like this: "Sitting on the dock of the bay, watching the tides come in." Friends, too many of us in life are sitting on the docks of our bays and waiting for our ships to come in. Sitting back and waiting on something to happen. Too many of us are sitting on the dock. The great singer Otis Redding made millions from the song he wrote, sitting on the dock of the bay, but you and I will never make millions or a million or accomplish anything sitting on the dock of our bay waiting on something good to happen. Waiting on our ship to come in. We must understand that in life, we must jump into the bay and swim toward our ship of opportunity. We have got to meet our ship halfway if necessary. Whatever it takes.

The Bible teaches us in James 2:14–25 that faith without works is dead. James was saying that it's not enough just to have faith. It's not enough to hope for something. It's not enough to wish something would happen. We must plan our work and work our plan in faith. We must use our God-given abilities to get the job done. We must get up with a desire to make it happen. There is a hero within each of us that has a great desire to get out and accomplish something great. Every one of us has a spiritual gift and/or a physical talent based on our personality and our calling.

Some of us can't get it done because we are too busy bragging to folks about what we are going to do. The Bible teaches us in Ecclesiastes 9:10 that whatever we set our hand to do, we should do it with all our might. Jesus said in John 10 that he came to Earth that we might have life and have it more abundantly. Never stop dreaming. We can do all things through Christ Jesus who strengthens us. The Apostle Paul put it like this: "We are more than conquers."

Some of us make the mistake of sitting around waiting on something to happen while others get up and make things happen. Oftentimes people are only a third as good as they think they are. Some of us are legends in our own minds not in our own time. One of my sayings is, "Don't tell me about the labor pains, show me the baby." In other words, don't talk about it, be about it. The Nike sports company puts it like this: "Just Do It." One of the famous sayings in the area of getting up and making things happen is: "If you're going to run with the big dogs you must get off the porch." Friends, it's time for us to get off the porch and make it happen. Faith without works is dead. In one of the accounts of the Gospel, where Jesus came to the disciples on the water, (Matthew 14:28-29), Peter did something the other disciples were unwilling to do. He put his faith into works. He understood that it was not enough to just sit and have faith. Peter rose up and stepped out of the boat onto the water and was literally walking on the water.

In other words, he put his action with his faith, and it worked. He was doing the impossible! Whatever we attempt to do in life, if we get out of our boat like Peter did and step out on faith, we can get out of the boat of mediocrity. Step out of the boat of fear. We too can achieve the impossible. We too can excel. We too can go where our critics say we cannot go, achieve what our enemies say we could never achieve. That which the haters say cannot be accomplished, in it all our Lord may receive the glory.

When I lost most of my eyesight as a seasoned pastor at the age of fifty-two, I felt defeated. I felt discouraged. I felt that it was all over for me. But then the Holy Spirit spoke to me and said, "You got to get up and go back to work and get off the dock. I am not finished with your life. There is still much that you can achieve in life. I am going to present more opportunities for you to advance the kingdom on this earth."

I must admit that at first I wanted to die, but I began to understand that I had to get off the dock and swim to the ship of opportunity. I began taking classes with the associations that help the blind to learn how to walk with a special stick. I began taking classes to learn how to type full sentences on a computer. This was very frustrating initially, but I begin to understand that God had open a door for me to walk through for his glory.

I can state to you today that by getting off the dock and swimming through the doors that God had opened, I now realize more than ever before that my life was not over. It had really just begun. I am now able to go on the internet and type full sentences on a computer. I am preaching the word of God and pastoring my churches although I am unable to read the

Bible (I study the Bible by audio) or any of my notes. I am planting new churches under the leadership of the Holy Spirit. In other words, God is accomplishing more through me in my physical blindness than he was when I had my sight. In closing, whatever the Lord is calling you and inspiring you to do in life based on the gifts and talents that he has rendered unto you, get off the dock, get off your behind, and get it done with his help.

Wherever God Is at Work, the Devil Is Not Far Behind
Chapter 11

Matthew 4

In life one mindset that each of us as individuals must be constantly aware of is that wherever God is doing work, our archenemy, Satan, the devil, is not far behind scheming to curtail or intercept the work that God is doing. Oftentimes the work that God is doing is within and through the lives of people like us.

Let me mention something about our number one enemy, Satan, the devil. First of all, he hates and despises you and me. If you are an individual that is striving to follow our Lord and Savior Jesus Christ, Satan hates, you. His number one objective is to destroy you. Satan, the devil, is our real adversary. The Greek word for Satan is *diabolos*, which means accuser. The scripture tells us that Satan, the devil, goes to the throne of God and accuses you and me day and night. The devil is real. The Bible tells us in Ephesians 6 that we wrestle not against flesh and blood but against principalities and wickedness in high places. A lot of folks don't take Satan seriously. What they fail to understand is that a lot of problems, whether they're in relationships, finances or even health, are often due to Satan, the devil, causing them behind the scenes. The devil is very intelligent. The devil is powerful. He is a spirit being that is thoroughly evil. He is the single-handed cause of the fall of humanity.

He defeated the first Adam in the Garden of Eden back in the book of Genesis. He caused one-third of the holy angels in heaven to rebel against our great father in heaven. He is the real enemy of God. He, the devil, is the leader of a host of other powerful spirit beings. They assist him in trying to defeat God's purposes. The Apostle Paul calls him the prince of the kingdom of the air (Eph. 2:2). The enemy will never make a frontal attack on you and me. He fights dirty. He will attempt to get to you and cause havoc in your life through friends, spouses, church members, work colleagues, children, etc. He will use whatever means necessary to bring defeat to your life.

We understand how real he is and his strategies from Matt 2:1-14, where Satan was behind Herod seeking to kill Jesus. In other words, God the father sent his son to save humanity from our sins and Satan tried to kill and destroy him before he could go to Calvary and the cross. No cross—no salvation for humanity. No cross—no reconciliation for humanity. Jesus came to undo what the first Adam failed to do, and that was to remain totally faithful to the word of God and to choose good over evil. Friends, even in your busyness of life, God is working to bless you. Friends, God has ordered your steps and ordained you to be very successful in what you are doing. God has set in motion a plan for your life to be a leader in your industry. Yet due to the fact the devil is striving to disrupt those God-ordained plans for your life.

The devil wants you to quit. He wants you to throw in the towel. He wants you to surrender to defeat and he wants you to wave the white flag. He speaks in your ear and tells you ha, John, ha, Terry, ha, Mary, you can't do it. You will never qualify for that award. You cannot achieve and produce those numbers. You cannot pass that exam; you are not smart enough to do that. You will never amount to anything. Your life is a mistake. You should have never even been born. I am here to tell you that the devil is a liar and the father of lies. You are not a mistake. The Apostle Paul inspired by the Holy Spirit put it like this in Ephesians 2:4–8, "Even before he made the world, God loved us and chose us in Christ to be holy and without fault in his eyes. God decided to adopt us into his own family by bringing us to himself through Jesus Christ." No mistake about it, no matter who you are, no matter how many mistakes you have made, your life is not a mistake. Our great God in Heaven had you in mind from the very foundation of time before he ever made the world. God loves you. That's why he also told us that we are more than conquerors. God is also faithful to finish the work that he has begun in you and me.

Friends, we must stay the course. We must be willing to finish the race. God is on your side. In Romans 8:31, it says, "If God is for us, who can ever be against us?" Also, remember Romans 8:28, which says, "And we know that God causes everything to work together for the good of those who love God and are called according to his purpose."

Friends, you can do it. You can do all things through Christ who strengthens you. You can get that degree and you can overcome that sin. Go about life, whether in your personal life or your business life. We need to recognize that Satan, the devil, is our number one enemy. We need to be aware of his strategies as it says in 1st Peter 5:8. Brothers and sisters, prior to losing 80 percent of my sight a couple of years ago, I was really busy with the work of the kingdom. I was pastoring multiple churches, overseeing seventeen pastors of churches in three states. I had just founded another church in the states of Tennessee and North Carolina. I had also just founded a new Bible College. I think this it's fair to say that God was using me in a profound way for his kingdom. But just as the title of this chapter states, when God is at work, the devil is never far behind. Even when we look at the fourth chapter of Matthew, we see that Jesus's ministry began in the Judean desert, where he had just been baptized by John the Baptist. He was beginning the work to establish the church and training disciples that became apostles after his death. But as usual here comes the devil. Folks, please keep in mind that if you are not doing the work of God, you probably will not have much trouble from the enemy. The trouble that you will have is the consequences of wrongdoing and wrong living, which will catch up with you. But when you are an ambassador for Jesus, living for him and working for him, the enemy will come against you harshly.

When I found myself really being moved for the kingdom's sake, the enemy attacked my eyes. Just like in the book of Job, where God said Job was a righteous man, yet he allowed Satan to attack him. God used Satan for his divine purpose in Job's life. However, at the end of the story God restored Job back, not to his original place, but with several times more than what he had before. It took me a while after losing my sight to realize that my story was similar, and that God had allowed the enemy to take my sight in order that he might work in my life in a profound way. He gave me greater spiritual sight so I could completely focus on his kingdom's work.

Most people through our churches have stated to me on many occasions, "Pastor, you may not be able to see much in the physical, however your vision in the spiritual is greater than it has ever been before." What I am saying brothers and sisters, is that even though the enemy is at hand, and even though when God is working through you the enemy will be nipping at your heels, we serve a God that will make everything come out for our good if we learn to trust him. However greater is he that is in us than he that is in the world. If you will stay the course, God will give you the victory. God will give you the strength and power to finish the race.

Undignified Praise
Chapter 12

2nd Samuel 6:14

Brothers and sisters, every day that we get up we should be thankful to our Lord Jesus for another day of life. He is the one that puts a roof over our heads, puts clothes on our backs shoes on our feet, and puts food on our table. However, the enemy, Satan, wants to steal our praise. And the reason that he wants to steal our praise is that, if you do your biblical research, you will find that his original name was Lucifer. The Prophet Ezekiel tells us that when Satan was Lucifer, he was an archangel. The Bible teaches in this book that he was created perfect and with beauty. He was given dominion over the earth. However, in his original role prior to his assignment on the earth, he was the leader of the praise team in heaven. His job was to lead the divine choir in giving praise to the Father and the Son and the Holy Spirit in the third heaven. However, in Ezekiel 28 he begins to get puffed up; in other words he became prideful. And then he began to want to exalt himself above God's throne. And he was cast to the earth by the archangel Michael. This is what we call Lucifer's flood found in the first chapter of Genesis. So the reason the enemy cannot stand praise of God is because this was his original job and purpose.

Brothers and sisters, any time that you are going about your life without doing what you are called to do by God just to make some money, you will be miserable. Satan is miserable because he is not working within God's plan. We need to look daily at our lives to see if they are operating within God's plan for us.

Here in the text of 2nd Samuel 6, we find that King David has just received back the arch of the covenant that was stolen by the Philistines. The Bible says that he was so full of joy and thankfulness that he began to dance and to praise and to give thanks to our Lord. He did not care who was standing around looking. He did not care what his neighbors thought. His whole attention and focus was as ours should be when we take up praise for God. Everything else should be tuned out. We should not have our minds on what we are going to do next or who we have to call. Our focus when we are in praise should be totally consumed with Jesus Christ. Sisters, it's not time to worry about your nails when it's time to praise. It's not time to worry about your dress, and it's not time to worry about your makeup. Men, it is not time to worry about your tie or suit or when the NBA basketball games or the NFL football games are coming on TV. Folks, it is not time to worry about where you are going to eat. Here in the text, King David was focused only on who his God was and what his God had done in allowing Israel to recapture the ark of the covenant. Yet David was ridicule because of his praise.

He was ridiculed by Saul's daughter, Michal, David's wife. In this story you will find that David used multiple musical instruments. He was so focused on his creator god that, in this episode of praise, he tore his clothes. And just like Michal, we have others standing around us when we get into our praise saying that it does not take all that. However, they may not understand what you have been through. They may not understand from where God has brought you. They may not understand that you have just been brought out of the valley of the shadow of death. They may not understand that you almost didn't make your rent payment this month if it had not been for Jesus. They may not understand that your mother would have died if Jesus had not healed her. They may not understand that you may have been killed in an automobile accident a day earlier. They may not understand that you have gotten a job that you did not even have the education level to obtain because of God.

The Bible says David danced. We don't mind dancing in the clubs. We don't mind dancing at parties, so tell me what is wrong with dancing in praise. We don't mind getting all excited and jumping up at our sporting events, pumping our fists and waving our arms because somebody just hit a basket or because somebody ran a touchdown.

David was not worried about dancing at clubs or parties. He was responding to his God and what his God had allowed him to accomplish. Brothers and sisters, the Bible teaches us that when praises go up, blessings come down, and the Lord inhabits our praise. Undignified praise simply means what it says: that you are not concerned with looking dignified when it comes to praising our God.

We can learn a lot from King David in this story, and please keep in mind that David is the only person in the scriptures that almighty God speaks of as a man after his own heart. I believe that the reason for this is that King David was probably the greatest praiser in the Bible. He was not concerned about being cute. He was not concerned about what other people around him were saying. His whole focus was on showing his gratitude and thanks and love and adoration for his God. I believe that this is the primary reason that God makes this rare statement about King David. This is evident in the fact that David was the writer of much of the book of Psalms, which is mostly made up of praises of our God.

Finally, brothers and sisters, let's stay true to the words of the Bible: let everyone that has breath praise the lord. Please keep in mind that if you want to run the devil away, out of your house, out of your car, out of your business, out of your family, and out of your life,

let your praises go up and your blessings come down

and your enemy will flee.

He Got Up
Chapter 13

1st Corinthians 15:3-58

Folks, we are living in a world and in a time where there are many people that boldly proclaim that they do not believe in God. They believe that the Holy Bible is made up of fiction. However, there are many things, such as creation and rainbows after the rain (the Noah covenant), that points to our divine creator, God. Here in the Bible passage 1st Corinthians 15, we find that the Apostle Paul is dealing with individuals that not only did not believe in God but also did not believe in the resurrection. The Apostle Paul was making the argument that not only was Jesus the first born from the dead but all of Christianity hinges on the fact that Jesus was raised. He was arguing this fact against, most likely, the Sadducees, which was a religious group in Jesus's day that did not believe in the resurrection. Paul here is stating that if there is not a resurrection of Jesus, if he had not been raised from the dead, that means he is still dead and there is no hope of salvation. There is no hope of the second coming of Jesus. There is no hope of an afterlife.

Brothers and sisters, please understand that this is one of the number one strategies of the enemy, Satan, to discourage us. He does not want us to have any hope. Hope is the first cousin to faith. Hope means, in the Greek, an anticipation of something.

The Lord wants us to anticipate his second coming daily. To anticipate him delivering us, healing us, rescuing us, leading us, and bringing us out. Here Paul continues his argument, making it plain that if Jesus had not been raised, we just need to party because tomorrow we die. Brothers and sisters, wouldn't this be a sad occasion if the troubles that we face in this life are all for nothing? This is what the devil wants us to believe: that the work and the life that we live for Jesus is all in vain. All for nothing! But the devil is a liar, and the truth is not in him.

Paul continues to argue that not only is Jesus raised, not only did he get up on the third day, but he is coming again and sitting at the right hand of his father. And there is coming a day when Jesus will return to this earth to set up the literal kingdom of god. A time when every knee will bow, every tongue will confess that he is Jesus, the King of Kings and the Lord of Lords. Paul teaches us here that one of the last enemies that will be swallowed up is death. Paul puts it like this: "Oh death, where is thy sting? Oh grave, where is thou victory?" There is coming a time, he says, when there will be no more diabetes, no more cancer, no more emphysema, no more Alzheimer's, no more prenatal deaths, no more drive-by shootings, no more air plane crashes killing hundreds, no more drowning, no evil, but the fullness of the kingdom of God, which is the restoration of all things that were spoken of by the apostles.

Paul concludes this passage by stating that those of us who are born again will die as mortals but be raised in the resurrection to immortality. After being raised, we will not contend with flesh but have spiritual bodies that cannot take on diseases again. Just as when Jesus was raised, he had a spiritual glorified body. The other good news about this passage is that those who have died in Christ, your grandparents, your mother, your brother, your child, your father, your sisters, and your friends, at the resurrection, at the second coming of Christ, you will be reunited with them again in the kingdom of God. There is a time coming when there will no more political campaigns, no more races for the president, senate or the congress. There will be one president, one senate, and one king in all of the earth, and his name is Jesus, as told in Isaiah 9:6. His kingdom will fill the entire earth. Paul teaches us here that one of Jesus's greatest assignments on earth will be to deliver the kingdom up to the Father.

No wonder the enemy tries to downplay this coming event and this hope. Because it pictures a time when he will no longer be present on earth. The Book of Revelations teaches us that he will be bound and put into a bottomless pit for a one-thousand-year period. Finally, Paul says that we should be encouraged by these words and that this truth should inspire us and motivate us; because when times are tough and the midnight hours come, the hope of Jesus's coming should cause us to get up and be steadfast and immovable in Christ. He got up, and we can too.

Stop Putting Off for Tomorrow What You Should Be Doing Today
Chapter 14

Haggai 1:1-10

Brothers and sisters, how many times during our lives do we find ourselves procrastinating? We often find ourselves putting off something for tomorrow that we know we need to do today. Satan, the devil, oftentimes uses the art of procrastination to work against us. Oftentimes he uses this delay tactic to take us away from completing the tasks in our lives that need to be done. For example, we often start things that we don't finish. We start to clean up, but we don't finish. We start taking educational courses, but we don't finish. We're going to do some renovations to our homes, but we never get started or never complete the task. We're going to study the Bible more, but we fail to do this too. We make New Year's resolutions every January, and a few months into the year we are right back in the same place. We are going to lose weight, but we never get to it. We're going to eat better for our health, we're going to start exercising or join a gym, but that was two years ago. We're going to attend church more; we are going to ask the pastor what we can do to help more in the church, but it never comes to pass. We're going to begin college. We're going to finish our GED from high school, but we never start. The enemy even makes us think that we have more time left on the earth than we actually have.

Here in the text with the prophet Haggai, we find that the people are delaying building a house for the Lord. The Lord gives them a strong rebuke. He condemns them in a few different areas. Number one, he says they are too busy with their own agendas instead of concentrating and focusing on the real work, which is the Lord's work. He also states that they are carried away by their own lives. He asked them to consider their ways, or in other words, to examine themselves. He's stating that we need to examine ourselves and our lives to see if what we are putting off for tomorrow is more important than the things we are doing today. He also continues to rebuke the fact that they are caught up with the cares of life and things that don't mean that much. The things that they are doing are not productive. The things that they are doing do not amount to anything. The Bible teaches us in the Old Testament scripture that unless the Lord builds the house, the laborers toil in vain. That's why we see our lives and other folks' lives as unproductive even though some of them work hard. All we need to do is look back on our lives and see how far we have come. I promise you that if you are not busy going about your father's business, you will not be satisfied with what you have achieved in life. God says, "Unless the Lord builds the house, the laborers toil in vain."

What God is saying in that passage is the same thing he is saying through the prophet Haggai in the first chapter. He is instructing us that unless what we do is blessed by the hand of God and directed by God, it is futile. It is just like the principle of tithing. Most folks never understand the principle of tithing, and that's why they stay broke. This is why their finances stay in shambles. And if they only accept the word of God in the matter of tithing, putting God first in their lives and trusting him by doing what he says, he will provide for them. He states in Malachi 3:8 that he will bless us if we bring meat (tithes) into his house. He says, "I will open up the windows of heaven and pour you out a blessing so large you would not be able to receive it."

The definition of the word tithe is a tenth, or 10 percent. However, how many of us actually pay 10 percent of our income? How many of us has practiced this paying 10 percent of our income, out of every check? And then we wonder why what we do with our money is unproductive. It's like having a cup with a hole in it and still pouring drink into the cup, then wondering why we cannot fill the cup up. The Bible even teaches us to lean not on our own understanding, but in all our ways to acknowledge him (Jesus). The people here in this passage of Haggai were not only procrastinating in the building of God's house, they continued to make every excuse as to why they were putting off the building of the Lord's house for tomorrow and doing their own thing today.

Friends, what task, what job, what goal are you putting off for tomorrow that you should have done today? One of the proven ways to deal with procrastination is to first recognize this sin. We must admit that we have a problem in this area and then ask God to help us overcome it. Procrastination is the practice of delay. Throughout my life I have been blessed to have numerous accomplishments because of the blessing of the hand of God. I have often discovered that the best way to overcome procrastination in addition to prayer is to take one bite out of the task each day. In other words when you think about delaying a task, just go ahead and do the most difficult part of the task and get it over with.

Oftentimes the reason for procrastination is that there is a part of the task we don't like doing. For example, if you are selling a piece of real estate, you may like showing the property but hate to do the paperwork for the contract. You may want to go ahead and prepare the contracts if that's the most difficult part of your job. If I am a pastor, I may not like doing reports. I may want to delegate the task of preparing church reports to another leader in the church.

Finally, whatever goal we have set or whatever task is at hand, let's not allow the enemy to cause us to continue practicing delay tactics in our lives. Let's learn from God's indictment of the people in the book of Haggai. Let's not allow our own lives, the cares of this world, and our own agendas continue to put off for tomorrow what we all know we need to do today.

Let's Ask for Something Worthwhile
Chapter 15

1st Kings 3:7-11

Brothers and sisters, every problem that we encounter in our lives has something to do with wisdom or a lack thereof. What I am saying to you is that everything that is going wrong in your life or mine is caused by a lack of wisdom. The Apostle James states to us in James 1 that if any of us lack wisdom, let us ask for it from God. There are many definitions of the word wisdom. Some state that the definition of wisdom is knowing the difference between what is right and wrong. We will see in a minute what the biblical definition of wisdom is and what the Bible teaches us about wisdom. It is not the world's wisdom that I am speaking of, because the world we live in today does not have a clue what wisdom is.

The best definition of a wise person is someone that chooses to live by a high moral standard. This world does not understand morality. Satan, the devil, has such a profound negative effect on this world that he has caused the unraveling of its moral fabric. The Apostle Paul speaks of this in 2nd Timothy 3:1-5, where he states, "In the latter days, we will live in perilous times when people will call good bad and bad good." All we need to do is look at our own schools, neighborhoods, and communities, as well as all the negative news reports, to see and understand this fact.

I can testify personally that the many mistakes I have made during the course of my life have been due to a lack of wisdom in those areas. When I lost most of my physical eyesight over the past two-and-a-half years, some of the problems were due to choosing the wrong eye doctor. This was because of a lack of wisdom. I have made mistakes in parenting my children; although I believe I have been a good father, I have made mistakes due to a lack of wisdom. I can even admit to making mistakes in my marriage due to a lack of wisdom.

Brothers and sisters, wisdom is something that we should ask God for daily in our prayers. One of the things that I have learned in the latter days of my life is to lay the need for wisdom before God on a daily basis. I ask God each day for more wisdom in order to lead his people, and I ask him for greater wisdom in all areas of my life. The Bible teaches us in the book of Proverbs that wisdom is greater than rubies. In other words, God is saying we should seek after wisdom more than we seek after money because wisdom is more important than money.

I can also admit that I have committed financial blunders due to a lack of wisdom. If we are truthful, we can see these poor decisions all around us. How many times have you seen someone asking advice from Mookie and Pookie instead of going to the real source of wisdom to help with their problems? We see that Mookie's and Pookie's lives are tore up from the floor up, yet we still seek advice from them.

Another example is that in marriage, the Bible teaches us that a soft tone turns away wrath. However, how many times do we find ourselves raising our voices back toward our spouses and getting into a knock-down, drag-out type argument. This is an example of a lack of wisdom. We have been taught all our lives that being humble is the way. We know that God teaches in his word that he who exalts himself shall be humbled, and he that humbles himself shall be exalted. We have been taught throughout our lives that we need to set aside a little savings out of every paycheck that we get. However, how many can admit to the fact that we fail to do this time and time again? We have no emergency savings, some of us are in our fifties and we have basically no retirement. Friends, this is all due to a lack of wisdom.

Let's look at a passage in 1st King 3 and see what's going on. Here, King Solomon has been commissioned by God to build the temple, and he has completed the task. His father, King David, is dead. He has been chosen by God to assume the kingship of his nation. The Lord is pleased with Solomon and has asked him what he can give him. Solomon could have asked God for anything in the world. He could have asked God for greater riches. He could have asked God to eliminate his enemies. He could have asked God for a long life, but he asked God for wisdom. Here, the Bible teaches us that the definition of wisdom is to have an understanding heart to know what is just and the difference between right and wrong.

The Lord was very impressed by Solomon not asking for something for himself, and this is why I named the chapter. Let us ask for something worthwhile. What I am saying is Oftentimes we are always asking things of the Lord that are not that important. We ask God for a bigger house. We ask God for more expensive cars. We ask God for greater health. However, friends, we need to be careful to ask God for wisdom. Over the last few years, I have learned to include asking God for wisdom in my prayer life. I have made a lot of better decisions in all areas of my life since then. Friends, I wish I would have learned this simple truth many years ago.

So when we look at King Solomon, the Bible says that God granted his request for more wisdom, and he became the wisest man to ever live, other than Jesus. One out of every two marriages end in divorce in our nation. This is because we do not utilize wisdom within the scope of our marriages. I can guarantee you that if we would ask God for wisdom in our marriages and all of our relationships, then these negative statistics would decrease by a lot. Some folks get mad at their bosses and just end up quitting before they can find another job. What kind of wisdom is this? In the raising of our children we don't spend the proper time with them, yet we wonder why they learn bad habits from their friends, who are greater influences on because they spend more time with them than we do.

Now back to the story in 1st King 3. King Solomon was doing very well here in chapter three. However, if you continue to read the rest of King Solomon's life story, you will understand that he got tangled up with a lot of women who had pagan beliefs that corrupted him. This shows that even if we ask for wisdom and grow in wisdom, we have to put wisdom into practice in our lives. In other words, wisdom must be exercised. You can decide to lift weights to build your muscles, however, you must lift the weights to build the muscles. It is not enough just to have the weights. If you decide to build a house, you can purchase the lumber and the materials to build the house, but if you do not hire a contractor to put the lumber together in the building of the house, it is all in vain. In other words, it's not enough to have something if you don't exercise or put it into practice. In our national politics, the biggest problems with our congress and our White House are due to a lack of wisdom exercised by these individuals. True wisdom is also defined by simply obeying, staying true to, and applying the word of God to every area of our lives.

Finally, friends, if we ask God for wisdom on a daily basis and apply it to our lives, many of the problems in our lives will be solved. Let's keep in mind that most of the problems that we have come from a lack of wisdom. If we ask the Lord for wisdom, he will be faithful to grant it; therefore, many of the things that are lacking in our lives we can obtain by using and applying the proper wisdom. So let's be careful to ask of the Lord something that's worthwhile. Let's ask for more wisdom.

Keep in Step with the Spirit
Chapter 16

Galatians 5

Brothers and sisters, the Holy Spirit is the third member of the Trinity. He is God. There are three members of the Trinity, God the Father, God the Son and God the Holy Spirit. He is equal with God because he is God. They are three in one.

Oftentimes we have been taught incorrectly regarding the Holy Spirit. Some Bible teachers have taught that the Holy Spirit is some type of source of power that is extended from God. However, the Bible speaks of him as a spirit of comfort, a counselor, and a spirit of truth (just to name a few of his roles). The New Testament shows that when the spirit is mentioned in the Greek, he reveals to us that he is a person in himself. We can also pray to him just like we pray to Jesus and God the Father. The Bible teaches us that he is an encourager and comes alongside us in times of need. So let's be careful to give him his proper credit. He is an ever-present help. Here in the text we find that the Apostle Paul, speaking to the church at Galatia, instructs members regarding how they need to keep in step with the spirt. We can only keep in step with the spirit if we yield our members to the Holy Spirit, Paul said. Let me give you an example.

When we dance with someone else to some music, we cannot be doing the two-step while the other person is slow-dragging, because this would result in a very disorderly and ugly dance. If we are two-stepping, the other person must be two-stepping. If we are shagging than the other person must be shagging. If we are slow-dragging, then the other person must be slow-dragging with us. I think you see the point. If the Holy Spirit is leading us to the left, we should not be going to the right. If he is leading us to the right, we should not be to the going left. If he is leading us to stay at a job, we should not be leaving that job. If he is leading us to stop cursing, we should not be cursing. If he is leading us in one direction, we should not be going in a different direction.

So the Apostle Paul goes on to say that if we do not keep in step with the Holy Spirit, it can cause consequences or manifestations. He gives a list of sins that result from us not being led by the Holy Spirit. Let's take a look at them.

First, Paul states that there is a war going on internally in our bodies, minds, and hearts. He states that the Holy Spirit is at war in us against the flesh and that the flesh is at war in us against the Holy Spirit. Jesus mentioned in the Gospel that the spirit is willing, but the flesh is weak. He stated this prior to going to Calvary, while he spent time with a few of his disciples that he had brought along to give him moral support and encouragement. He went to pray for strength to complete his assignment, but when he came back at one point, the disciples were asleep. He asked why they couldn't stay up with him, then he stated that the spirit is willing, but the flesh is weak.

Now let's look at the list of sins that result from us not being led by the Holy Spirit. Number one is adultery. In this present age, we live in an adulterous society. Adultery is when someone is married but sleeping with someone other than the one they are married to. Paul goes on to speak about fornication. Fornication is defined as anyone that is having a sexual relationship outside of marriage. He speaks of idolatry. This simply means when we put something before God; that could be our jobs, children, grandchildren, or spouses—whatever we allow to take first place in our lives other than God himself.

One of the biggest sins in the Old Testament scriptures show that God set up kings to rule his people.

He goes on to speak of witchcraft. Let me take just a moment to elaborate on this category of sin. Satan, the devil, comes in and gets a foothold in our lives and even our children's lives by playing with witchcraft. I know some are thinking, "I don't mess with witchcraft," but let me explain, or in the words of an old farm boy, "let me shuck this down to the cob for you." Ouija boards, palm readers, and root doctors are all of witchcraft. All of these are of the devil. The Bible even teaches us that rebellion is like witchcraft. In other words when we rebel against our pastor, elders, deacons of our church government, or our bosses at our jobs, we are rebelling against God.

In the Old Testament, when Moses's sister Miriam spoke against Moses, God the Father was offended and struck her down with leprosy, which would have eventually killed her. However, Moses went to God and pleaded for her life, and the Lord listened to him and removed the sickness. We can see that God is offended when we go around in a rebellious fashion and talk against his leaders, work against his leaders, and backstab his leaders.

All too often we find this mess in the church. If you cannot agree with the pastor, go to him and sit down and discuss the problem. We are also able to go on our knees to God with our problems. However, we should not take matters into our own hands and work against the leaders of God.

Next, Paul speaks about wrath. The fact of the matter is that some of us cannot control our tempers. We have a problem with our anger, and some of us need anger management classes. I mean when we get hot, we will say and do anything! We don't care who hears us. We don't even care who sees us when our temperature gets hot or when we get mad. Some of us will curse, some of us will stomp our feet, some of us will throw things, and some of us will be ready to fight somebody when we get mad. Paul says this is a result of not allowing ourselves to be led by the spirit.

Next, he speaks of envy. Now this is when we see someone else prospering or progressing and we get an attitude about it. We don't even want to speak to the person, so we avoid them because we are jealous of their success or prosperity. Even church members have problems when Joe or Jane gets a new car, or when Jason and Susan get a new house, or when Mookie and Pookie get promoted at their jobs. Friends, this is shameful, especially in the body of Christ. As a pastor, I have even counseled married couples that were jealous of each other. When the other one started making more money it caused a problem in the relationship. The fact of the matter is they should be celebrating each other's successes. We all should be celebrating one another's successes and victories.

Jealousy is of the devil. One of Satan's primary faults was that he was jealous of God. God the Father had given him dominion over the earth, but that was not enough. He wanted to be God. He didn't want the earth, he wanted the universe. I only touch on some of the highlights of this sin list, but Paul concludes by saying that those that lived a lifestyle with these sins will not enter the kingdom of God.

Paul concludes this section of the text by stating that if we walk in step with the Holy Spirit and we yield our members to be led by the Holy Spirit, the fruits of the Holy Spirit will be evident in our life. On top of the list is love. Now in the Greek, the love that Paul is speaking of is *agape*. Agape love is not a human love, it is a love that can only result from the Holy Spirit working through our life.

In the thirteenth chapter of 1st Corinthians, Paul speaks about love. He states that love is not rude, that love is not puffed up, that love is patient, and that love is long-suffering. Love is kind, and love is not self-serving. In the Gospel, Jesus never did one miracle for himself. Every miracle that he performed was serving someone else. We can all learn a lot from this last statement. He went on to say to his disciples that the greatest among you will be a servant.

Next, Paul speaks of joy. The Bible teaches us in the book of Psalms that the joy of the Lord is our strength. He then speaks of peace, and we have learned in the Bible that even in times of trouble or grief, Jesus is our peace. This is the type of peace that is not just the absence of war. This is a peace that will strengthen us when we can't find peace anywhere else.

Paul concludes the chapter by stating that when we yield our members to keep in step with the Holy Spirit, there is no way but up for us. The Bible teaches us that Enoch walked with God. In other words, he had a deep enough relationship with God that the Bible says he walked with him. When we walk with someone to exercise, we usually have a great relationship with that person. Paul is alluding to the fact that we should have the same relationship with God the Holy Spirit, that we may walk with him and keep in step with him. If we do, we will be blessed. Our lives will have many victories. So brothers and sisters, as we get up and live our lives each day, let's keep in mind to keep in step with the Holy Spirit.

Fatherhood Under Attack
Chapter 17

Romans 8:15

Friends, in this nation of the United States of America, the role of fatherhood has been diminished. Even manhood has been diminished.

Let's begin with manhood. Satan, the devil, has influenced our society in even asking for neutral genders; in other words they don't even want to distinguish between a male and a female. They don't even want us to teach our young sons not to play with Barbie dolls. They are teaching today that it is ok for the young male to play with whichever doll he wants to. This is why we have young male teens wearing tight pants and even female clothing like dresses—because they are not being properly taught how a male should conduct themselves in a different way than a young female. The Bible teaches us in Genesis 2 and 3 that God almighty created a two-gender humanity. The

Bible says he made them male and female, not male and male, not female and female. Our father in heaven created us in a way that there should be a difference between a male and a female. As fathers, it is our jobs to teach the difference between manhood and womanhood.

Now let's take a look at fatherhood. All the statistics suggest and confirm that when a female child grows up with a strong father figure in the home, she is twice as likely not to end up working as a prostitute. She is also twice less likely to end up working as a stripper. She is twice less likely to get pregnant as a teenager. Let's look at the males. When a male grows up in the household with a strong father figure, he is as twice likely to stay out of trouble with the law. He is twice as likely to graduate from high school. He is twice as likely to go on to college after high school.

In the African American community, all the statistics confirm that there is an epidemic of major proportions regarding single parent households. In other words, the father does not live with the mother. The confirmation of what I'm teaching here is that the prisons are filled with young African American males due to this epidemic. Now let me be clear, there are some mothers in African American communities that are strong enough that they have raised good sons and daughters, but in everything there are exceptions to the rule, and I thank God for these strong mothers. However, I'm speaking in general terms.

Let me talk about my own story. My father was an absentee father. He would not work or hold onto a job. He cheated on my mother with other women all the time. He was abusive with my mother when he was in the house. So of course a household is better off without a father like this. My father also abused alcohol, and yet my mother was a strong enough a person to raise the two sons and a daughter that came from this union. My younger brother is a deacon in the church and my sister is a leader in her local church, and both of them are very hard workers and have succeeded. You know my story, but let me make this perfectly clear: all three of us would have been better people if we would have grown up with a strong father figure in the home.

My mom implored my uncle, her brother, to help raise us and give us a strong father figure. And I can tell you that it really helped. If it hadn't been for my uncle, I probably would have been a negative statistic in somebody's prison. He refused to allow me not to work and to hang out on the street corners with my friends. He taught me that if a man does not work, he also should not eat. We cannot blame the problem in the African American community on the women. We have to blame it on our fathers because they have not done what they are supposed to do. It is my prayer that some of our fathers will read this book and be encouraged to take back their God given role.

In Romans 8:15, the Apostle Paul, inspired by the Holy Spirit, teaches us that we have a God from whom we can learn how to be fathers. Let me explain. Our heavenly father is our protector, he is our provider, and he is also our encourager. Statistics show that our daughters receive their self-esteem from their fathers. In this chapter, Paul talks about how we can cry out to our father, "Abba father!" In Aramaic this means *daddy*. You have to earn the title of daddy in this world. A child just doesn't call you daddy if you are not closely involved in their life. I had so much resentment for my father because he abandoned my mother and his children and did not provide for us financially. You know that it is terrible when a fifty-four-year-old man cannot remember anything that his father gave him, but he did not give us anything as far as clothing, cars, money, or material possessions.

It took many years for the Lord to work with me to forgive my father for the way he abandoned his children. As I mentioned before, I would be a lot better man than I am today if I would have had a strong father figure in my life. Fathers, we have an incredible job and role in the family. The meltdown of the family unit in our society has come from us not doing our jobs. How can we as fathers have a child or children and not want to be involved in their lives? What kind of mess is this? I have always wanted to be the opposite of my father, to do the exact opposite of the things he did. He abandoned us, so I wanted to stay with my family. He drinks too much, so I didn't want to drink like that. He was never involved in our lives, so I wanted to be closely involved in my children's lives. In the body of

Christ, I believe as pastors that we have a great job to do in addressing these issues through ministry and mentoring these young people who do not have strong father figures. Let me make one thing very clear. We have some very good African American fathers that have stayed the course and mentored and provided for their children in our country and our communities.

Finally, fathers let's teach our young men about how to be men. Let's work with our mothers and help together to teach our daughters how to be women. Let's stand up and take back our God-given roles, because the Bible teaches us that we are the priests in our family. Let's change these negative statistics regarding the single-parent households in our African American communities. Let's be the protectors, the providers, and the encouragers of our children. Let's show this world what it really means to be called DADDY.

Be Aware of the Thief
Chapter 18

John 10:10

Brothers and sisters, Jesus teaches us in John 10 that he came that we might live this life more abundantly. He also teaches us that the thief, which is Satan the devil himself, comes to kill, steal and destroy.

Let's take a few moments and focus briefly on abundance. The word abundant means plentiful, which means there is no lack, there is more than enough. In other words, it is Jesus's desire that we have more than enough. Here he is speaking of having plenty spiritually, having plenty physically, monetarily, and regarding health. Some Christians believe that it is some kind of a badge of honor to be poor. The Bible says that the poor will be among us, but it does not say that we have to be one of them. Here Jesus makes it clear to us that he wants us to succeed in life and to have the best of life, both spiritually and physically.

The problem with us is we don't plan to fail, we fail to plan. The Bible says people perish because of a lack of knowledge. The Bible also teaches us there were many rich godly men in the Bible. For example, Abraham was richer than rich and is known as the father of the faithful. The nation of Israel came from Abraham. Job is another example of a very rich individual in the Bible.

I am not saying it is God's plan or desire that every human being be rich, because some of us cannot handle being rich. If some of us woke up one morning and had riches we could not even focus or put God first in our lives. Some of us would be over in European nations on vacation, drinking piña coladas on the beach, and eating great food, and never set foot in a church. Some of us would drink ourselves to death. Some of us would eat ourselves to death.

Now let's get back to the enemy, the thief, Satan, the devil. The Bible says he comes to kill, steal, and destroy. Let's deal with the killing and destroying first. The devil wants to kill your name and your reputation. He wants to slander you. He wants to destroy your testimony before men and women. If it were possible, the enemy would kill and destroy you and I as we speak. The Bible teaches us in the book of Job that God placed a hedge around Job. He allowed the enemy to attack Job, take his family and his riches, and even strike his health. However, God would not allow him to kill or destroy Job. Let me explain something. Satan must check in with God to bring any attack on you individually. The enemy must have the permissive will of God in order to do anything against us.

This should make each of us feel secure and safe—knowing that the devil does not have the power to destroy us or kill us because of the hedge that God has placed around us. Friends, whatever tribulation or difficulty is going on in your life, be assured that somewhere in the midst of it the thief is somewhere close by. Job understood this matter, yet he trusted in his God so much that even after attack, after attack, after attack, at the end of the story, Job stood up and said, "I know that my redeemer lives." And the Lord restored to Job more than he lost.

Now friends, a thief is someone that comes and takes something from us. I want to explain something to you. I hear people even in the body of Christ stating things like: "The devil stole my car." The devil did not steal your car, you didn't make your car payment. They state: "The devil took my home." The devil didn't take your home, you didn't pay your mortgage. Let me take another step to clarify: the devil doesn't want your stuff. Let me show you what the devil wants to steal.

The devil wants to steal your joy. The devil wants to steal your spiritual focus. The devil wants to steal your assignment that the Lord gave you on earth. The devil wants to steal your faith. The devil wants to steal your peace of mind. The devil wants to steal your marriage. The devil wants to steal the assignment of your church and wants to tear down your church and your pastor. This is why we see so much havoc in the body of Christ among our churches. All of us have witnessed the tearing down and the dividing of our local churches. In some cases, a pastor has an affair, and then it becomes public and a church that was thriving in the spirit is divided and torn down. We have all witnessed this. And sometimes the church rebounds and is restored, and sometimes it is never the same again.

The devil wants to steal the armor that the Apostle Paul speaks of in Ephesians 6. In this chapter Paul speaks of us getting up each day and putting on the full armor of God. I mean he speaks of the breast plate of righteousness. The helmet of salvation. The belt of truth. The shield of faith.

Let me talk about the shield for just a moment. The shield is a defensive weapon. When someone attacks us, the shield is designed to defend us in our everyday lives, as the enemy attacks us with fiery darts. These darts may come in the form of slander, health issues, mental issues, discouragements, financial problems, marital problems, child rearing problems, and others. Our faith guards us from these attacks when we totally trust in our Lord for help in these matters. The Bible teaches us in Hebrews 11:1 that faith is the substance of things hoped for and the evidence of things not seen. We may not be able to see our way out or even feel our way out. There may not be any evidence that these attacks are coming to an end immediately. However, we trust in the one God and lean and depend on Jesus the Christ. He is the one that continues to watch over us and encourage us to get up and continue the fight. We must be careful to put on the full armor each and every day to defend against the attacks of the enemy.

In a war you cannot win just playing defense, however. You must also go on the offensive. The Bible teaches that the offensive weapon is the sword. In the Bible, the sword is the word of God. We must defeat the enemy with the word. So if you don't know the word, that's why your tail is being kicked around the block in your everyday life. Some of us don't have the common sense to understand that. If your life is far from great, it is because you are not a student of the word. I can run the enemy out of my home and out of my life by fighting him with the word of God, the sword. When the devil attacks me (and he does daily because I am a minister of the Gospel—make no mistake about it), all of us Christians are being attacked by the devil; however, he attacks the ministers of the Gospel, especially the pastors, more often.

Satan stole my eyesight two and one-half years ago. The Lord allowed him to steal it because he had to check with God in order to attack me in this way. And what he meant for evil, the Lord turned it into good. Friends, Satan is the source of sickness. It is his desire that we all be sick. The Lord is not the source of sickness, the enemy is. It is the Lord's desire that we all be abundantly healthy. Now we have to help him in this matter by eating properly, taking our medication if needed, exercising when possible, stimulating our minds by reading positive information and books, and allowing our minds to dwell on positive things in life. Satan attacked my eyes in order to destroy the ministry that God placed me in; however, God in his great power has used me more mightily with the loss of my physical sight than he did when I had two good eyes.

Finally let's make no mistake about the thief that comes to kill, to steal, and to destroy. Friends, what has the thief stolen from you? Has he stolen your peace of mind? Has he stolen your joy? Has he stolen your finances? Has he stolen your marriage? Has he stolen your good health? Just like Job we can regain what the thief has taken from us. If we fight the enemy with the offensive weapon that God has provided for us, his word, and have total faith in the one that has all power in his hand, the Lord will be careful to restore us with more than the enemy stole from us. Let's realize that he does not want our stuff unless we are using our stuff to bring glory to Jesus Christ. So let's be careful to avoid and be aware of the thief.

Marriage for Life
Chapter 19

Genesis 2:24
Matthew 19:7-9

Folks, the institution of marriage is in heavy decline due to the fact that the enemy, Satan, has attacked the family, as I mentioned in chapter 16. Marriage is an institution that has been attacked as a stepchild. It is something that the enemy has attacked in such a way that it now has a negative connotation. For example, it is common to see divorce today. It is not even thought of in a shameful way as it was in past years. The statistics teach us that one marriage out of every two in America ends in divorce.

One of the biggest problems with marriage in America is there is no long-term commitment. Satan has influenced the downfall of marriage to the point that people want to shack instead of getting married. They treat marriage like a car dealership. Let me take this relationship on a test drive by shacking (shacking is living together without being married). Like when we buy a car, we test drive, we kick the tires, we hit the accelerator, we hit the brakes, and if the car does not do what we expect it to do, we take it back to the dealership after the test run. If we have purchased the car already and it begins to not live up to our high expectations, we then take the car to another dealership and trade it in. Even when we drive the car long enough and it has lived up to our expectations but the new car smell wears off, we then consider taking it and trading it in for a newer vehicle that has more bells and whistles.

We have diminished the institution of marriage to mirror the way we purchase and drive these vehicles. The marriage does not live up to our expectations, so we want to trade in our spouse. the marriage does not have the freshness of the day that we made the commitment, so we want to try someone else. However, our lord, Jesus Christ said in Matthew 19:7 that marriage is supposed to be for life. He emphasized this to the audience he was speaking to, even when they brought up that Moses had permitted bills of divorce in the Old Testament for the men of Israel who wanted to put their wives away. Jesus went on to state that this was not the original intention for the institution of marriage.

Jesus went on to explain that marriage is not like a car dealership, where you can trade them in when you want to or when they don't meet your expectations. He stated that the only time you were able to divorce a husband or wife is if they committed adultery. The Bible teaches us in another place that when a spouse dies you are automatically released from the marriage covenant. In 1st Corinthians 7, the Apostle Paul speaks of the rare occasion where the Bible permits us to leave a person that does not wish to dwell with you. These situations are exceptions to the rule; however, it was Jesus's intention originally that marriage be for life. I believe that is clear because Jesus expects a lifetime commitment in the institution of marriage.

This is the reason that many do not want to get married. They would rather live in sin, the sin of fornication. Young women in our nation and community oftentimes allow the man to sample the package without purchasing it first (marriage). Friends, if I am able to go in a grocery store and sample the food prior to purchasing it, why would I purchase the food at the end if they would allow me to eat all the food I can eat? The famous singer Beyoncé even made a good song when she says, "Put a ring on it."

Brother and sisters, we are living in a time where the word virgin is a bad word—a virgin being someone that has not had any sexual relationship with anyone. They are saving themselves for the institution of marriage with their husband or wives. Just like Satan has tried to tarnish the word Christianity, he has also tarnished the word virgin. There was a time when the word virgin really meant something incredible, and this was something every man was trying to find and take home to mother and father.

Friends, I have been married thirty-four years and I have counseled married couples and couples that want to get married for twenty-three years as a pastor. I can tell you that I have dated my wife since high school, when she was fifteen years old. She was so young that her parents would not allow me to take her on a date outside of the house. I had to date her by sitting with her at her parents' home. I believe that one of the only ways that we have remained married for thirty-four years is due to the fact she was a virgin when I met her. I promise you that this characteristic about her was so important to me that I wanted to marry her from day one, and I was only seventeen-years-old when I met her and began to date her. By her being a virgin and had not been with other men made me realize that this was the woman I needed to marry. This fact of her virginity made me fall deeply in love with her more than I would have if this had not been the case. I can tell you that she has been an incredible mother, grandmother, and a very good wife. I believe that if she had been with other men, this marriage would not have lasted this long.

What am I saying? Am I saying when a woman is not a virgin you should not marry her? No, I am not saying that. I am saying that in a Biblical sense, a marriage has a better chance of survival when we do it the right way. I am saying that it takes three for a marriage to work. The three are the husband, the wife, and Jesus Christ. Lord knows we have had problems over the years, and the only way that we have succeeded so far is that we kept Jesus in the middle of our marriage. It is true that a marriage that prays together stays together. We have many times gone to our knees together and asked the Lord to save our marriage. I believe from the bottom of my heart that my wife was chosen by God to be my help mate in my ministry and the assignment that God has given me on earth. One of the greatest things that I will say is that God has given both of us a commitment to each other in the Holy Spirit. Jesus has given us the resolve to work at this marriage.

This takes me to one of my final areas of this chapter. Marriage is not supposed to be easy. Marriage is hard work! Everything worthwhile in life takes sacrifice. Marriage is about compromise. Compromise means that it cannot always be your way, and it cannot always be her way. You have to learn to meet in the middle. We have to learn to have the heart to do what we need to do in order to please the other person, and you cannot be selfish and self-centered and expect your marriage to work.

For example, I know that my wife loves to shop. I mean I can mention taking her shopping, and she lights up and smiles. I mean she gets so excited that she usually has to use the bathroom before we go. No, I don't like to shop. I can go into a store and find a suit of clothes within fifteen or twenty minutes, and then I'm back out the door (this was before I lost my sight). So when I know that my wife is struggling with something or something has happened in her family or at her job, and something has her discouraged with life, oftentimes I will suggest that we go to the store and look around in the clothing store that she likes. Although I do not like to shop, I am willing to endure it in order to make her happy and to please her.

Husbands, this is a small example of the type of thing we need to be doing to help please our wives. Something else may please your wife or cause your wife to light up or be encouraged, and it is important that you find out what that is so you can do those things for her on a consistent basis. This will go a long way in helping your marriage grow in a positive direction.

As husbands, we also should not expect our wives to cook every night. We should at times cook ourselves or take them out to eat. In other words, we should wine and dine them at times. We should plan romantic dinners for them. Husbands, we should take them out of town to nice places at times even if we have to cut the financial fat off our budget. Even if we have small children, we should arrange for a babysitter at times in order to spend an evening with our spouses alone. Every week, we should set aside a date night where we spend quality time with our spouse.

Men, we should also dress to impress our wives. We should also practice good hygiene. We should brush our teeth, we should comb our hair, we should wear clothing that they like to see us in. We should dress and appear in a way that keeps their heads turning. We should dress in such a way that they are attracted to us. We should even splurge and spend money on a quality men's cologne so that when we walk by them, we smell incredible. We should exercise so that we keep our bodies in good shape.

Finally, let me give you another area of great instructions and this instructions for the husband and the wife. Counseling is not a bad word! I know that our society has made the word counseling out to be a bad word; however, most successful, long-lasting marriages have included counseling at some point. Sometimes we need counseling even when things are going well in order for the marriage to remain strong. If we decide to go to counseling, it should be with a Christian counselor who has the same type allegiance to the word of God as we do.

In closing, no matter where your marriage is, if you have not signed the divorce papers your marriage is not over. The enemy, Satan, will tell you that it is at a point of no return, but the devil is a liar, and remember he comes to kill, steal, and destroy. The Lord Jesus can save your marriage if you both are willing to seek godly counsel and if you both are willing to humble yourselves before the mighty hand of God and allow him to lift you up. If you both are willing to submit yourself to what the word of God says and teaches about marriage; if you both are willing to admit that you are wrong in specific areas and willing to change them; if both of you are willing to understand that Jesus Christ says that marriage is for life, your marriage can be turned around by the one who created marriage from the beginning, our lord, Jesus Christ.

Marriage and Respect
Chapter 20

1st Peter 3:1-7
Ephesians 5:25

Brothers and sisters, one of the greatest weapons that our archenemy the devil has used against the divine institution of marriage is the word disrespect. If we look at the marriages in our country that have failed, I guarantee you that, if we were to shuck it down to the cob, we would discover and uncover that one of the primary causes of its failure would be disrespect.

Many of us remember the funny comedian Rodney Dangerfield. He was famous for his saying, "I get no respect." Most men in America within the scope of marriage can state the same thing. This is a problem within our marriages in this country, where the husband is not given his proper respect in the home. For example, there are times when wives speak to their husbands worse than they would speak to the dog or cat in the house. There was a lady many, many years ago that used to work for me, and her desk was outside my office. I knew when she was talking with her husband and when she was talking to her children by the tone of voice that she used.

Wives, it would help you to understand that your man would do a lot better by you and would operate and function in a more positive manner if you show him the proper respect. Now the word respect in the common dictionary is defined as adoration of an induvial due to their qualities. However, this is not the definition that the Bible teaches us about the word respect.

Before we look at the Bible scriptures that speak of what is expected as far as respect is concerned, let me make a couple of things very clear. A wife needs love just like a man needs respect. A wife, in addition to love, needs security. She needs the husband to be the provider and to make sure that the mortgage is paid, that the light and water bills are paid, that there is food on the table and clothes on her back, and that her children are taken care of if they are still small. She needs to know that she has something dependable to drive. She needs love and security! Husbands it is our responsibilities primarily to provide for our wives. I mean, there is nothing wrong with her having a career. A lot of women today desire to have a prosperous career, and this is great because God has given them gifts and talents to be used in the context of their lives. The world needs their gifts and their talents to make it a better place. However, don't get it twisted; it is the man's primary responsibility to provide for his wife. If anyone needs to work a second job it should be the husband.

Now the husbands needs respect. They yearn for respect. They live for respect. I am teaching you today in this chapter under the inspiration of God the Holy Spirit—if you have any chance of turning your marriage around, it will be done with love and respect.

Wives let me make one thing clear as we continue. In the second chapter of Genesis, we find account of God's creation of the heaven and the earth, the animals, and the vegetation, and he said everything was good. However, he finally saw that man needed something greater than animals and vegetation in order to be fulfilled, that it was not good for man to be alone. So God went on to perform a great divine surgery. He put Adam to sleep, took his rib, and created a woman. The Lord goes on to say that for this reason, a man shall leave his mother and father and join to his wife. When Adam saw the woman, he responded that he had never seen anything so beautiful. He was astonished by what God had created to help him. The Lord stated that this was his help mate.

Oftentimes in marriage, the woman becomes a hurt mate rather than the helpmate she was originally created to be. The first woman was one of the main reasons that Adam failed in the garden after the Lord had told him which tree to eat from and which not to eat from. Notice that in this scene in the third chapter, we find that the serpent does not approaches Adam he approaches the woman. Now God gave the instructions to Adam and not the woman because Adam was the leader of the home and she was not. The Apostle Paul states that the woman was deceived, but Adam was not. So disrespect in the home began in the garden.

The way the woman should have conducted herself when the serpent approached her was to say, "My husband did not teach me what you are saying." The wife should have gone and gotten her husband and allowed him to hear what the serpent was saying; however, she took matters into her own hands.

Wives, let's be careful and prayerful to show the proper respect for our husbands. Adam was also wrong in this account. When the wife attempted to give him the fruit from the wrong tree to eat, he should have refused it. The Lord gave him the instructions about the trees. He had no excuse for accepting the fruit that he knew was from the wrong tree. He should have stood up in his house, put on his big boy britches, and explained to his wife that God has told them which tree to eat from and they were going to stay faithful to the word he had given. Look around Eve, can you not see what the Lord has given us and blessed us with? We dare not go against this loving God who has given us so much and knows what is best for us.

Now let's go to the fifth chapter of Ephesians. In the Apostle Paul's writings in this chapter, he teaches that the wife is to respect her husband and be subject to him as the church is to Jesus Christ. Now we know that the Bible teaches us that Jesus Christ is the living head of the church. He goes on to teach us that husbands are to love their wives as Jesus Christ loves the church. The Bible teaches us that Christ gave himself for the church. He went to Calvary and died for all of humanity. If you understand anything about the Bible, you know how much Jesus Christ loves his church. The church is the body of Christ.

At the end of Ephesians chapter 5, Paul does not only make it clear that wives should have great respect for their husbands and husbands should have great love for their wives. He also teaches us that husband and wife should submit one to another. He is saying, yes, the wife should respect the husband, and yes, the husband should love the wife, but at the end they both should compromise with each other. It cannot always be one way.

Finally, I want us to take a look a 1st Peter, chapter 3. Here we find that our Lord Jesus has used another apostle to write about the divine institution of marriage. Peter begins in verse 1 speaking of the deep respect that wives should have for their husbands. Now women, I really want you to understand this. Peter begins by stating that even if our husbands are unbelievers and do not practice the word of God, we should still show them the proper respect. Peter goes on to say that a godly woman that shows her husband the proper respect in the way she talks to him, in the way she acts toward him, and in the way she carries out his instructions, can win him over to Jesus Christ with her conduct. Peter goes on to say that women who practice this are the daughters of Sarah, Abraham's wife.

Now husbands, here Peter also teaches how we should have and show great love for our wives. Men, notice that both the Apostles Paul and Peter harp on the fact that we should love our wives, because men have trouble showing love to their wives. Peter goes on to say that we should treat our wives with tender love because they are the weaker vessel. In other words, they were created by God as weaker than we are.

This has nothing to do with their intelligence. I want to go on the record as saying (and this may make some men mad) that in counseling marriages over the years, I have found the woman in a marriage is often more intelligent than the man. And the Lord who created them understood this when he made the woman subject to her husband in the word of God. It is not because she is inferior. Husbands and wives let me be clear. The word of the living God here in 1st Peter chapter 3 and Ephesians 5 states to us that respect is unconditional and that love is unconditional. Unconditional means what it says; there are no conditions. For example, men I can't love my wife only when she does good things. I am expected by Jesus Christ to love my wife unconditionally. When she is up, I need to love her. When she is down, I need to love her. When her hair is good or bad, I need to love her. When she has makeup on, I need to love her. When she has no makeup on, I need to love her. When she has gained weight, I need to love her. When she has lost weight, I need to love her. When she cooks, I need to love her. When she does not cook, I need to love her. When she does not feel like having intimacy, I need to love her. When she needs encouragement, I need to encourage her. The Lord knows that I have made plenty of mistakes throughout my thirty-four years of marriage, but I have always tried to learn from them.

Wives, Jesus Christ expects us to have unconditional respect for our husbands. Let me explain what this means. Doing counseling sessions, I have often heard women say, "If he would do this, or if he would do that, I would respect him more." Again, unconditional respect means there is no condition on the respect. The only thing that God expects us not to do is go against his word in order to please our husbands. The Bible teaches us that we should obey God rather than man. If our husbands are not asking us to go against the word of God, we should follow their instructions and show them the proper respect. This is what the Apostle Peter and Apostle Paul were alluding to in Ephesian 5 and 1st Peter 3.

Wives, let me help you understand that you can have the husband of your dreams if you would only show him the proper respect. I would challenge you wives to just try this: begin today to speak to your husband with great respect. Act toward your husbands with great respect, and I promise you that your husband will begin to change for the better. There have been more than one couple that were just about to sign the divorce papers, and the wife began to practice the principle of showing great, godly respect toward her husband. Then the husband began to turn around and show her the great, godly love that God expects, and their marriage was saved. This has happened numerous times in the context of my pastoral ministry.

Finally, husbands and wives, don't let the devil fool you into thinking that there is someone better on the other side of the fence. It doesn't matter who you marry, there will always be a struggle between two human beings in the context of marriage. Men, we are expected to set the example in our marriages. Let's begin by showing our wives unconditional love and treating them with tender care as the weaker vessel. Let's remember what Peter says: that our prayers will be hindered if we do not show the proper love for our wives. Women, beginning today let's accept the challenge to show our husbands the proper unconditional respect that Jesus Christ inspired his two

Apostles to write about.

Lost My Sight, Gained My Vision, His Grace Is Sufficient
Chapter 21

2nd Corinthians 12:7-10
2nd Corinthians 5:19

Brothers and sisters, in this closing chapter, I would like to share with you my personal story regarding the loss of my sight. For over two decades, I have been a successful pastor and a successful business owner. My success in the business world allowed me to travel around the world. With two good eyes, I have been blessed to see places like London, England; Paris, France; Rome, Italy; Helsinki, Finland; St. Petersburg, Russia; Stockholm, Sweden; Madrid, Spain; Maui, Hawaii; and Monte Carlo, Monaco. These are just some of the places that I have visited and seen with my own eyes.

However, at the age of fifty-two, I began to have problems with my sight. I went to an eye doctor that told me, after he examined my eyes, that a little medication and some laser surgery would correct the problem. At the time, I was still driving during the day, at night, and even in the rain. The problem was that the particular doctor that diagnosed me initially did not accept my insurance, so I continued to search for a different doctor and was referred to one. I went to this doctor and he told me much of the same thing as the first doctor; that my vision problem could be corrected with a couple of laser surgeries. So I went and had the surgeries done, and I noticed that instead of improving, my vision ended up getting worse. I went back to the doctor and inquire about this, and he stated to me that sometimes it takes a little longer for the eyes to heal with some patients. So weeks went by and then months, and my vision continued to get worse.

Now friends, it is very difficult to be a pastor and lose your vision. The first problem I began to think of was, if I lose my vision, how can I drive to visit the sick? How can I get to church? How can I continue to fulfill my responsibilities at the church? I also began to wonder, How would I study the word of God? How would I prepare my notes to preach if I couldn't read my notes? How would I be able to support my family? All of these important matters began to flash before my eyes.

I have understood that I was called to be a minister of the Gospel since I was a little boy. My mother has mentioned this on many occasions to me, "Son I knew as a child you were called to be a minister of the Gospel." My mother went on to say that Satan, the devil, has been trying to destroy me since I was a small child. She stated that when she was carrying me in pregnancy, a car ran into us, which could have threatened a miscarriage. She then went on to tell me that at the age of eight years old, which I remember that I was hit head on by a speeding drunk driver while I was on a bicycle. I have also had a few situations just several years ago. I was sitting in traffic on one of the busiest highways in our state, and a car hit me in the back without even putting on breaks. The officer said he hit me going approximately 65 mph. I was in an SUV, and it caused my vehicle to flip three or four times. I ended upside down and had to have physical therapy rehabilitation for several months.

I say these things to make the point that when we have been given an assignment on earth by Jesus Christ, the enemy will pull out all stops in order to stop us from completing our assignments on earth. Now friends, my sight continued to get worse and at the age of fifty-two, I was declared by two eye doctors to be legally blind. Now, just as I suspected it would, my nightmare come true. I was unable to read the words of the Bible. I was unable to prepare sermon notes because I could not read them. I could no longer drive myself to visit my sick and shut in congregants. I was at a point of my life where I really did not want to live, because I felt like the very thing that God almighty called me to do was over. But I want to tell you friends, that whatever you're facing today, there is a way out.

Let me tell you the rest of my story. Jesus Christ, much like he did for the Apostle Paul on the road to Damascus, came into my room and told me that my life is far from over and that his grace was sufficient for me. He told me that he was going to do a greater work through me than he ever had before. He began to prepare sermons through me without my having to use notes. He began to preach his word through me better than he ever did, according to my church, when I had two good eyes and was using notes. In other words, I don't use notes by his power. He began to inspire me to get an audio Bible so I could study the word through audio. He placed some of my ministers around me to take me to visit the sick, and when they are not able to take me, my wife takes me to visit the sick. And he has also provided me with an administrative assistant to help me and drive me to the places I need to go. The Lord has also used me to start a Bible College to equip his saints for the works of righteousness, teaching them the word of God. It is connected through accreditation to over two hundred other Bible colleges in over thirty states in the US.

I want to say to you that I lost my sight, but I gained my vision. I can see Jesus Christ far better today than ever before. My relationship with him has increased tremendously. My intimacy with my savior is closer than ever. Now, we know that Jesus Christ has put a hedge around his people to prevent the enemy from destroying us, however, he will allow the enemy to attack us at times in order to take us to higher spiritual ground. I do not believe that I could have written this book through the inspiration of the Holy Spirit if I had not gone through what I went through.

What are you saying pastor? I am saying that sometimes the suffering that the Lord allows us to go through is for our good. Sometimes what does not feel good is for our good. In Romans 8:28, the Apostle Paul instructs us that all things work together for the good for those that love God and are called according to his purpose. Notice that he says all things, not some things, but all things work together for our good. I am stating to you, friends, that we need to keep these words in mind as we live our everyday lives and struggles. I realize now more than ever before that what I am dealing with—the loss of my sight and my other struggles—will all work together for my good. Because it is God's will that we be shaped into the image of his son Jesus Christ. Whatever you are facing, Jesus's grace is sufficient for us. Through his grace he will help the worst situations get better in due time.

Don't allow anyone to judge you. There are some who, when you face calamities and disasters in your life, will say that you have done something wrong. Now in some cases this may be true. However, in Job chapter 1, the Bible teaches us that Job was a righteous man, yet he lost everything. He almost lost his mind, but at the end of the story, God totally restored Job and gave him more than he originally had. In John 9:1–5, there was a blind man that had been blind since his birth. The disciples asked Jesus, "Rabbi, which one sinned, this man or his parents?" Jesus responded and said, "Neither this man nor his parents sinned. For this man was born blind for the glory of God." In other words, our father in heaven allowed this man to be blinded so that his works of righteousness and his glory might be manifested in the man. And therefore, sometimes we are called to face conflict and tribulations in order to bring glory to God. Even Job's friends tried to tell him that he probably was committing some type of sin, however, this was not true. The Lord just wanted to know whether, if Job lost it all physically, he would still remain faithful to his God. Job passed the test.

Brothers and sisters, in the words of the Apostle Paul, I boast in the Lord in my infirmities, and I'd rather suffer these things that Jesus Christ might be magnified and exalted and that others might come to his saving grace because they see the work that he is doing through a handicap individual. Glory be to God!

Finally, I want to simply sum up this chapter like this: I may have lost my sight, but I have a greater vision for the work of the kingdom. I am able to see my savior face to face better than ever before. I can see him within my spirit and within my heart. Brothers and sisters, whatever you are facing today, don't give up, don't quit, because the Lord is moving you to higher ground.

The Bible teaches us that even Jesus Christ was made perfect by the things he suffered. We are saved by grace through faith in Jesus Christ himself. When he was dying on the cross, after he was beaten and bruised for our iniquities and before he gave up the spirit he said, "It is finished." And what he meant by that in the Gospel is that he had completed the work and the assignment that his father had sent him to do. He had redeemed all of humanity from the death penalty. We were all sentenced to hell, but his finished work on the cross has allowed us the opportunity to accept him as savior and place our names in the book of life, as told of in the book of Revelation. In 2nd Corinthians 5:19, the Apostle Paul states that after we repent, the Lord no longer holds our sins against us.

Be of good cheer my brothers and sisters, Jesus has overcome the world, and he has an assignment for you. Find out what that assignment is. He has given you spiritual gifts and talents to advance the kingdom of God on this earth; there is no greater calling than that. It is my sincere prayer that this book, that I believe is written under the inspiration of the Holy Spirit, will help you become a greater soldier for Jesus Christ.

The Invitation
Chapter 22

One of the important events that President Abraham Lincoln scheduled every week was attending Sunday evening church service. One evening when the President came out of the church following the service, the driver of his carriage asked him, Mr. President, how was the service? President Lincoln replied, "It was a good service, however, the preacher failed to do something. He failed to extend an invitation to the congregation that would allow them to accept Jesus Christ as their Lord."

Friends, I want to extend to you today an invitation to make Jesus Christ the lord of your life. I want you to repeat these words after me:

Lord Jesus, I repent of my sins. I understand that you died for me on the cross. You spilled your blood, and you allowed your body to be broken as a sacrifice to redeem me from the eternal death penalty. I believe that you not only died for me, but you rose on the third day. I accept you this day as my personal Savior, and I want to make you lord of my life forever.

Now, friends, if you read this aloud, I believe that you are now a born-again Christian. You have passed from eternal death to life. Now please, find a good Bible-teaching, Holy Spirit–filled church to attend on a regular basis.

Please write to us and let us know that you accepted Christ. You can contact us by writing to us at PO Box 516, Marion, SC, 29571. You may also look at our website at

www.theamazinggracefellowshipofchurches.org

Acknowledgments

All proceeds from the sale of this book will go toward preaching the Gospel of Jesus Christ. It will also go toward feeding the hungry, clothing the naked, and ministering to the homeless.

Biography

Dr. Blakeney was born September 10, 1964. He grew up in Charlotte, North Carolina. He graduated from Central High School, Pageland, South Carolina, in 1983. He received his undergraduate degree from the University of South Carolina in 1987 and received his Master in Theology in 2012 and his Doctor of Divinity in 2014 from All Nations Bible College and Seminary in Myrtle Beach, South Carolina. Pastor Blakeney was ordained into the ministry in 1996 within the Grace Communion International Fellowship. He founded the Amazing Grace Fellowship of Churches in November 2014 and has planted new churches in Murfreesboro, Tennessee; Whiteville, North Carolina; and Marion, South Carolina. He is currently the president and bishop of the Amazing Grace Fellowship of Churches. Dr. Blakeney is also the president and founder of Amazing Grace Bible College and Seminary.

He has been married for thirty-four years to Wanonia Myers Blakeney. They have three children, Kashonta, Dale, and Ladaisha. They have six grandchildren, Trevon, Kaylonee, Kaden, Kash, Kashori, and Kya. They have two sons-in law, Bryant and Reginald.

Made in the USA
Middletown, DE
31 January 2022

60129710R00106